D0336610

DUSTY

DUSTY

DUSTY HARE
with David Norrie

FOREWORD BY BILL McLAREN

Queen Anne Press

A Queen Anne Press BOOK

© David Norrie 1985

First published in 1985 by
Queen Anne Press, a division of
Macdonald & Co (Publishers) Ltd,
Maxwell House, 74 Worship Street,
London EC2A 2EN

A BPCC plc Company

All rights reserved. No part of this publication may be reproduced, stored
in a retrieval system, or transmitted, in any form or by any means, without
the prior permission in writing of the publisher, nor be otherwise circulated
in any form of binding or cover other than that in which it is published and
without a similar condition including this condition being imposed on the
subsequent publisher.

British Library Cataloguing in Publication Data
Hare, Dusty
    Dusty Hare.
    1. Hare, Dusty   2. Rugby football
    players — England — Biography
    I. Title   II. Norrie, David
    796.33'3'0924   GV944.9.H3

ISBN 0-356-10637-3

Typeset by Cylinder Typesetting Ltd, London

Printed and bound in Great Britain by
Hazell, Watson & Viney Limited
Member of the BPCC Group
Aylesbury, Bucks

For my wife Lesley, who has had so much to put up with over the years – and not only because of rugby – and accepted most of it without complaint; for my parents for showing me the good life; and for Donna and Christopher, our two children, who made going on tour such a terrible wrench.

Acknowledgements
I would like to thank David Norrie for his invaluable help and advice in putting this book together and the many photographers who have captured my trials and tribulations all over the rugby world. I am also grateful to all those that have given me a helping hand over the years, especially Chalkie White and the rest of the Leicester Tigers.

CONTENTS

FOREWORD

Since the days when catch, clearance and tackle were his key watchwords, the full-back's role has undergone considerable change especially in the area of attacking play. It remains, however, a role in some isolation, calling for nerve, patience and cool judgement and it is those qualities, when set alongside high levels of skill, that have enabled William Henry Hare to make such an auspicious contribution to the Rugby Union game.

I have vivid recall of the first time I saw the young Hare in action. I had been called in at the eleventh hour to cover, for BBC Television, the Midland Counties East versus Fiji match at Leicester on 7 November 1970. I had never seen the Fijians until the morning of the match. Not only did most of them look alike to me but I faced the ordeal of coping with names like Naucabalavu, Tokairavua and Tikoisuva! Imagine my horror, too, on discovering that the East Midlands would not be numbered 1 to 15 as was customary, but would carry the letters 'A' to 'O' on their backs. Even worse, no sooner had I got used to that than 'P' arrived in the person of a youthful replacement called W. H. Hare of Newark, Notts, Lincs and Derbys. Having left Magnus Grammar School just three and a half months previously, he was only 17, had played two representative games and came on as a centre. One was not to know then that he was to become England's most-capped full-back but I remember how that youngster settled to his task with no fuss and any amount of determination as the Fijians put on the pressure to win 24-14.

Any full-back who can claim three wins and a draw, and only two defeats, from six major international appearances against Wales has to be something special. But there is much more than bare statistics behind my admiration for Dusty Hare, and this makes it such a pleasant chore to provide a foreword to a book which surely will make fascinating reading, having been written by one who has known the ups and downs of rugby fortune and taken them all with good grace and good sense. He has never seemed to me to 'flap' when the flak is flying all around. Whether he has just sent a goal-kick wide that he knows he should have slotted, whether he has just misjudged the drift of a bit of enemy aerial bombardment or whether he has been caught off balance by a whizzing enemy sidestep, he never seems to turn a hair. Like the top professional golfers, he has the capacity for putting his disappointment behind him as he prepares to take on the next challenge. The same appears to have been the case in the numerous high points of a thoroughly satisfying and successful career. Even when he was in the process of scoring all of England's 19 points against Wales at Cardiff in 1981, he had that same phlegmatic approach to the turn of events.

Perhaps it all has to do with being a son of the soil where acceptance of the rough and smooth is so much part and parcel of farming life. But it has always seemed to me that Dusty Hare has set for the younger rugby adherents an admirable example in field behaviour and attitude. Having provided commentary at some 15 of the 25 major internationals in which he has played I cannot recall ever having seen him commit one questionable act or give the slightest hint of dissent or bad sportsmanship.

Whilst he would not claim to have been the quickest full-back in the realm of Rugby Union internationals, folk have tended to underrate the keen sense of anticipation and clever positioning that have made him a potent force as an intruding or counter-attacking full-back, in which regard I have fond memories of his try against Wales in 1981 when, with intuitive judgement, he just materialised to take a scoring pass from Paul Dodge as John Carleton made a feint run. So it did seem strange, admittedly from the distance, that the British Lions in New Zealand in 1983 did not make wider use of Dusty Hare in view of his impressive haul of 88 points in the only six games he played.

Undoubtedly he has placed himself in rugby legend as one of the greatest goal-kickers of all time. There are very few men in the history of the game who have struck an average of 10.4 points over 25 internationals. In much the same way as golfers find their longest drives appearing to be effortless Dusty Hare would send a place kick soaring high and long with a lazy swing of the right leg and impeccable timing, all of that on a sure foundation of intense concentration. I have been lucky enough to be 'on the air' when some of the most dramatic winning goal-kicks have been made under the keenest pressure. I'll never forget how that controversial line-out incident led to Brian McKechnie's crucial penalty goal giving New Zealand victory by 13-12 over Wales at Cardiff in November 1978. Scots have joyous recall of that monumental goal by Andy Irvine from miles out on the right touchline – the very last kick of the game – that brought Scotland victory by 16-14 over England at Murrayfield in 1974. Those were kicks that brought the weight of history on to the shoulders of the kickers. The same could be applied to what I consider the finest of many pressure kicks landed by Dusty Hare. There was high drama at Twickenham on 16 February 1980. England and Wales were unbeaten in the Championship. Paul Ringer of Wales had been ordered off by referee David Burnett. Yet Wales had taken an 8-6 lead with a try by Elgan Rees and there were only three minutes to go. In injury time William Henry was called forward to attempt a penalty goal from the most demanding angle out towards the right touchline. England hadn't beaten Wales for six years. You could have cut the tension with a knife. But the lad did not falter. He hit it plumb and all England rejoiced. I have always reckoned that that kick really won England their 1980 Grand Slam. Even as a neutral observer I have to admit to having experienced a flicker of pleasure that things had turned out right for William Henry who, in every sense, before that and since, has been an adornment to the great game.

BILL McLAREN

11

1
HERO OR VILLAIN?

After all the hours spent on the training field, in cars and coaches going to matches, on planes touring abroad, sweating and toiling – individually or in a group – in all weathers, my entire rugby career will probably be remembered, by most people, for less than ten seconds of action; a few quick steps and a well-practised swing of my right leg. It is a movement I have made a million times, but never more dramatically than on 16 February 1980, when my penalty from the right-hand touchline gave England a 9-8 victory over Wales at Twickenham in the dying seconds of the match.

Such is the lot of the goal-kicker; the supporters slapping you on the back one minute and stabbing you the next. Rugby may be a team game – and is probably the greatest – but I'm out on my own when that ball has to be put between the posts for victory. There have been some glaring sporting misses over the years. Golfer Doug Sanders will never forgive himself for missing that three-foot putt at St Andrews which allowed Jack Nicklaus to steal the 1970 British Open. Nor will Don Fox forget the sliced kick in front of the posts in the last minute of the 1968 Wembley Rugby League final that left Wakefield Trinity runners-up. I wouldn't put Jeff Astle's miss-kick with an open goal against Brazil in the 1970 World Cup in the same class – such errors are mere reactions and the chance is gone before the culprit has time to consider the effects of being off-target. Not so the golfer on the green or the penalty-taker. Nobody could forget seeing the photograph of South African full-back Jack van der Schyff with his head hung in shame after his conversion drifted away from its target, giving the 1955 British Lions the first Test, 23-22.

Fortunately, I haven't felt like that too often. I don't think I've ever missed a really simple chance to win a match, although I'm sure, having said that, someone will dig up some obscure game in

COLORSPORT

COLORSPORT

The moment that proved something to those who said I was not a pressure kicker, saved Steve Smith's England career and made the 1980 Grand Slam possible – my third penalty against Wales.

which I let a side down. A year after that victory over Wales, I had a penalty chance in injury time to turn a 21-19 deficit into an England win at Cardiff, but the kick was just out of easy range and by hitting the ball too hard I managed to hook it. Still, I had scored the other 19 points myself! I remember making kicks near the end of matches to enable England to sneak home in Japan (1979) and South Africa (1984). Obviously, my kicking has been a factor in England's Championship and with Leicester's John Player Cup successes, but often those penalty points are only a reward for the efforts of others. Other times I have been making amends for earlier lapses, never more so than in the Midlands' historic victory over the All Blacks in the autumn of 1983. True, I put us in front with a penalty from my own half and then sealed New Zealand's fate with an even longer dropped goal, but the record books make no mention of the simple penalty chance I hooked from nearly in front when the scores were 13-13. Being the goal-kicker does at least allow you the chance to redeem yourself.

Of course, you need confidence in your own ability, but you don't kick week-in, week-out at senior club level for over a decade without knowing what you can and cannot do. There are days when the ball just will not travel between the posts – as I demonstrated in the wet of Murrayfield in 1984 when I missed six kicks out of eight – but experience will tell you how to put things right. You also know that the law of averages is in your favour; being a recognised kicker means those around you also have the confidence to allow you to come through a bad patch without chopping and changing the kicker. Other days you are 'hot' and the ball is drawn over the bar as though by remote control. Sometimes a different pressure can get to you. One penalty, near or far, is just part of the job – often the realisation of that responsibility hits you afterwards. But knowing that every kick must go over because the team is unlikely to score any other way is tough. Playing for England was sometimes like that. I wasn't shaking in my boots when England were awarded that final penalty against Wales in 1980. Like Steve Smith, I was only grateful we had another chance of victory after seemingly throwing the game away a few minutes earlier. As Steve had played a major part in Wales' two tries that day, not only did England's Grand Slam hopes fall squarely on my shoulders, but so probably did the future of his international career. Still, I was glad of the chance and, despite the wide angle, felt confident in making the kick. Those people who can't bear to watch or can't imagine what it is like to be under such intense pressure forget that I'm only doing my job. They tend to look at it as though it's they themselves that are having to take the kick or sink the 12-foot putt. It's never easy, of course, but I, like Sevvy Ballesteros, am a 'professional'. I might not be paid for kicking penalties for England, but that's what I'm there for and if I can't do that, there's little point in me being there.

That is a view the England selectors have taken on numerous occasions. Officially, I was dropped five times by England – a record jointly held with Mike Davis and John Finlan, although Huw Davies seems to be catching up fast. In my case it might well have been six times because I heard that I had not been included among the three full-backs for the 1984-85 season – they were Marcus Rose, Chris Martin and Nick Stringer – when I announced my retirement from international rugby. As far as the public are concerned, I got in before the England selectors, but in real terms it was 'six and out' for William Henry Hare, better known as Dusty.

2

FROM HEROES TO VILLAINS

The British Lions' tour officially went wrong for me on 11 June 1983 when I struggled off with a back injury in the match against Southland. Exactly 52 Saturdays later, England – and I – were staggering to our worst-ever international defeat, against the Springboks in Johannesburg. Sandwiched in between was England's first home win over New Zealand for nearly half a century which totally flattered to deceive as our Five Nations Championship challenge soon afterwards crumbled into disaster. The tour to South Africa merely confirmed our position as also-rans. A year to remember – almost equally, a year to forget. A lifetime's rugby squashed into 12 months. At first glance, those weeks included all I could have asked for. A final ambition was achieved in making the British Lions party, then the following summer I was packing my bags again for my first England tour against an International Board country. In between came victories over the All Blacks for the Midlands as well as England, and my next game for my country – the 100th Calcutta Cup – saw me pass Bob Hiller as England's most-capped full-back. Then 14 points in Paris took me past the 200-mark for England and the magical 5,000 in my career. It was even a great year for my club, Leicester. When prop Steve 'Granite' Redfern ran on as a replacement for Colin White during the Irish match, the Tigers' representation became a 'Magnificent Seven'.

All this, yet Dusty's still complaining. Well, I'm sorry, but milestones and personal records count for little, especially when England are at the bottom of the pile. We have an abundance of rugby talent – even the Welsh, Springboks and All Blacks admit this. 'If you ever get your rugby organised . . .' has always been their great fear. But England don't, and predictably the players and coach continue to labour as failures. It would help to face reality. How about this from the Rugby Football Union's report at the 1984

AGM: 'a great success on and off the field'. They were describing our South African humiliation! At the same meeting, the proposed plan for a national merit table was thrown out at the instigation of Yorkshire. You wouldn't have found many of England's leading players cheering that night.

A Year in the Life: No Breaking the Irish Connection

The full story of the British Lions tour to New Zealand, with the Test whitewash, is recalled later in this book. Suffice it to say I returned home a disillusioned man. I had rattled up 73 points in my first four matches and seemed to have a good chance of making the second Test team when I was injured at Southland. That was the halfway mark of the trip, but the Lions' selectors called on me only once more, for the match against Hawke's Bay towards the end of the tour, during which I damaged my collar-bone.

I had a few weeks off when I got home as I needed to work out where I stood – I felt I had deserved more of a chance in New Zealand. The biggest blow had come when I wasn't selected against Canterbury, the mid-week match before the third Test. That confirmed my role as an also-ran, a 'dirt-tracker', all the more painful and obvious as the Lions took to the field without any recognised goal-kicker – Ollie Campbell and Gwyn Evans were also in the stand. Not surprisingly, the Lions paid the price, and I might as well have been assigned to one of the supporters' trips. Back on the farm I was left to wonder where my future in rugby lay. Lo and behold, the All Blacks, for once, came to my rescue. The aftermath of the Falklands War had led to the cancellation of New Zealand's tour to Argentina, so a visit to England and Scotland was arranged instead.

A Year in the Life: Revenge for a Few Gallant Englishmen

I was only half training by the beginning of September, but watching the first XV on the second Saturday whetted my appetite for the fray yet again. Despite my earlier plans to be absent until the middle of October, it was first team duty for me after one match against Harlequins seconds. That was the only way to get stuck in and prove I was still the best around, at least as far as England were concerned. There's no better test than the almighty All Blacks.

Leicester were playing well and the Midlands enjoyed a good warm-up match at Moseley. On the Saturday before the Midlands met the New Zealanders, Leicester sneaked a win at home against Cardiff. Both sides scored four tries in what was probably one of the best club matches I've ever played in. There were about 12,000 there and it's the only time I've ever played club rugby when the entire crowd has stood up and applauded the two teams off the field. The more traditional will be aghast at such a tough rehearsal only a few days before a crucial tour game, but it's the best way to prepare for rugby at the highest level. What is the point of players taking part in 'tea-party' games before internationals? Going from a joke to international rugby can't be good for you. The harder the rugby, the sharper you are on the field. That's one of the reasons there should be club league tables – then we might produce players fit to compete for England.

As the Midlands prepared, one familiar face was missing – that of coach Chalkie White. He'd been with us for so long that it was going to be interesting and just a little strange to see how we coped, and how new coach Martin Green dealt with us. He had a different approach, which was a good thing because you couldn't try to follow a man like Chalkie. Martin had a good attitude towards the players, and, together with captain Peter Wheeler, he worked the forwards into shape. Peter was the stronger of the two, and generally Martin let him take charge, going along with what he wanted and adding his own thoughts where and when necessary. Peter, too, had had a raw deal from the 1983 Lions' selectors, not even making the trip when realistically he should have been the captain. That had been England's fault as much as the Lions'. Now here was his perfect chance to laugh last and longest.

On the afternoon of the match you could sense the unity in the team and Martin has to take a lot of credit for that. Peter and I weren't the only ones with something to prove. Clive Woodward had found about as much favour with the Lions' selectors in New Zealand as I had, while Paul Dodge had found none at all. After nearly 80 years of visiting the UK, the All Blacks were preparing to play their first-ever match under floodlights. New Zealand had arrived without any of their front five from the summer Tests, but their replacements were experienced and had done well against the

Lions. We were not fooled. Beating the All Blacks is always a hard task; their record speaks for itself. They don't lose easily, and these particular tourists weren't going to let themselves down either.

The match was over in a flash. I missed a couple of kicks early on, but after I converted Steve Holdstock's try midway through the second half the Midlands were back on level terms at 13-13. But before long I was hoping the Welford Road ground would open up and swallow me – I hooked wide the simplest of penalties. No wonder Peter Wheeler instructed me: 'Put it down there' when, shortly afterwards, we got a penalty in our own half. I knew it was within my range and told him I wanted to kick it. We had a little argument but when Peter saw I was determined he gave in. As the ball sailed over the bar, we exchanged a smile – me, because I'd redeemed myself, Peter because he'd allowed himself to be swayed by my persistence. There was still a lot left to be done, though. A couple of minutes later, Murray Mexted hoofed the ball down-field after covering for his full-back. I caught the ball in my own half, took a few steps and hit the sweetest dropped goal of my life. Over it glided – I'll always remember that kick because I don't think I'll ever do it again! All we had to do was hang on for ten minutes – but ten minutes can be an eternity when the All Blacks' pride is at stake. Our forwards, and especially the back row, did not let us down, despite some inspired running from New Zealand captain Stu Wilson.

Welford Road erupted on the final whistle. The Midlands had become only the 14th side to lower the All Blacks' colours in 231 matches in Britain. We hadn't let the All Black forwards roll round and smash their way through as they'd done against the South of Scotland; after watching that game, we knew we just had to put them on the deck. Nobody demonstrated that better than the young Nottinghamshire flanker, Gary Rees, as he cut down wave after wave of New Zealand attack. It was a victory that was bound to put many of us in the England team for the Twickenham international 11 days later. After our poor showing in the 1983 Championship, there were question-marks over a lot of selections. England had a good chance of beating the All Blacks. The North and London had pushed New Zealand hard, and only the South-West were disap-pointing: considering the number of good players they have, their

BOB THOMAS

Peter Wheeler – still smiling, but missing some of the teeth that have been kicked in by the England and British Lions' selectors who ignored his undoubted leadership qualities.

21

COLORSPORT

Ignored by England and the Lions, this happy Leicester trio of Paul Dodge, myself and Clive Woodward have just completed the first half of a winning double over the All Blacks.

record against touring sides is ridiculously poor. However, they did redeem themselves with a 12-12 draw against Andrew Slack's Australians in 1984.

Although the 1983 England skipper John Scott was in the side, Peter Wheeler got the captaincy he'd long deserved. 'Brace' should have been given the job a long way back, even before Bill Beaumont. For England, the build-up was similar to that of the 1979 match against New Zealand when the North had beaten them a week before the international. That victory had turned sour with the selectors making a couple of silly decisions. This time all 15 players felt – and it always helps – that this was the best England team available. The training went well under our new coach Dick Greenwood. We had first come across him when an England XV met Canada in the pouring rain at Twickenham. Our new coach had been pleased with the way we coped with those conditions and worked hard for our win. My first impression of Dick, which will always remain, was that we should have doffed our school caps before seeing the teacher. Dick has a fetish about fitness. But international rugby is not about fitness, it's about organisation and making sure that all 15 players know what is going on. The selectors should know about a player's condition and if he isn't fit, then he shouldn't be on the international scene. Dick sent out a schedule and recommended a programme of training. On the farm it's hard to say 'I'm just going out for a half-hour run'. I don't think Dick is that hard pressed at Stoneyhurst College, where he is assistant bursar – he can probably spare the time.

But Dick learned as the season went on. I know England had a disastrous Championship and South Africa was even worse, but what do you expect from a coach who has hardly any experience at senior representative level? Whether he lasts the full three-year cycle or is pushed to the wayside like Willie John McBride is in the lap of the committee men. Why is a man who hasn't learned his trade given the top coaching job in England? How ridiculous it is to expect him to learn the hard way in one exhausting season of international rugby. If Dick didn't bring out the best in us, it was only because he was adapting to his new surroundings like the other newcomers to the squad. At Leicester Graham Willars, too, found it difficult in his first year, and not only because he was following

Chalkie White. But in the 1983-84 season, his second, Graham was tremendous and Leicester did very well.

Our forwards performed magnificently against the All Blacks, but although we kept the game tight and in their half, maintaining intense pressure, the New Zealanders still didn't make many mistakes. For all our domination and possession, England were rewarded with just one rampaging try from about two yards when the 'Marquis de Colclough' – as Peter Wheeler dubbed him afterwards in succession to Prince Obolensky – crashed over from a line-out. Because of our poor 1983 Championship, added to the fact that England hadn't beaten New Zealand at Twickenham since Obolensky scored his two tries in 1936, we were determined to get a win. However, we all knew that the rugby probably wasn't going to be particularly enjoyable as far as the spectators were concerned.

The press labelled us 'Bloody Heroes'. John Carleton was led off after being tackled by Bernie Fraser – J.C. later said that he thought he'd been thumped by a piece of lead piping and that his leg was broken. It was a careless charge, typical of Fraser the previous summer. But it wasn't a dirty match – if the All Blacks wanted to be dirty they could maim somebody – though it was certainly over-physical. The All Blacks wanted to leave a few trademarks, especially as they had become frustrated: 'OK, you've played us and beaten us, but we're not going to let you walk all over us as well'.

Paul Simpson had a courageous afternoon on his England debut; he was like a roaring Roman gladiator. His display epitomised the game – Twickenham was an emotional place that day and Paul played his heart out for his country. Yet I don't believe he played as well as some people made out; he wasn't the answer to our blindside flank problems and couldn't produce it on the next occasion. Scrum-half Nick Youngs was everybody's 'man of the match', but his performance was largely due to the magnificent platform he had to play behind; a scrum-half couldn't have had it any better with all eight in the pack going forward, pulling in even the most seasoned All Black loose forwards. While most of England got carried away, predicting another Grand Slam, a few of us who'd seen it all before realised that the victory was nothing special and would have little relevance to the Championship, especially as England missed the first weekend and had an 11-week wait before facing Scotland. So we had beaten the All Blacks and beaten them in the way we had planned, but it was by no means a conclusive success. Most of us went into the final trial fairly complacently, knowing full well that, barring a total disaster, the same XV would all make the Calcutta Cup.

A Year in the Life: Not Even George Orwell Foresaw This!

The traumas of the summer were behind me now; I was playing rugby, winning rugby – and that against those I hadn't been given a chance against on the Lions' tour. Two victories over the All Blacks in less than a fortnight make up for a lot of disappointments. Peter Wheeler had belatedly stated his case in the most conclusive manner and showed that his sense of timing was again spot on, this time as an author as well as a striker of the ball. His book *Rugby From the Front* had just been published and those two victories did wonders for the sales, leaving a memorable final chapter to be written in a future edition. In retrospect, the selectors' inspired decision to use the bulk of the Gloucester pack in the Rest team in the trial may have backfired. It seemed to knock a lot of the confidence out of the senior forwards; after dominating the All Blacks, the eight were never the same in the Championship, not once gaining any supremacy.

Not playing on the first Championship Saturday doesn't help. Normally you start level, but if you begin on the second weekend against opponents with one match under their belt, win or lose, you are at a disadvantage. Again it comes down to sharp, competitive rugby; it's not such a major problem for the other four countries because their international men have regular, tough contests. But our preparation was a shambles; there was a dreadful weekend at Bisham Abbey where we trained on frozen ground. Dick asked too much of us to work all day and then go off on a four and a half-mile run at the end of it. I'm sure a professional football coach wouldn't do that to his players a week before a big game. After all, a player only has to get himself fit for 80 minutes of activity. So many of the team had aches and strains. 'Brace' had hardly played since the All Blacks match because of a broken thumb and both the second rows were absent. 'Dodgy' was missing, too – more permanently – because of a broken leg sustained at Blackheath. We'd gone there in December with a very impressive record but had returned well

COLORSPORT

John Carleton – J.C. – a special friend who doesn't look too happy after being 'tackled' by New Zealand winger Bernie Fraser at Twickenham in November 1983.

beaten. I'm afraid the boys just weren't geared up for that game. Blackheath must be one of the worst grounds to play on; the changing-room, shower and bath facilities leave a lot to be desired.

Our preparations for England's 100th game against Scotland didn't improve once we had crossed the border. I should have known the writing was on the wall when Terry O'Connor of the *Daily Mail* did a big profile of me a couple of days before the game. 'The most influential Englishman on the field on Saturday' was how he described me – I certainly was, but not in the way he'd expected! We worked out at Easter Road, Hibs' soccer ground; the session was all higgledy-piggledy. Then we were out again on Friday morning; there was snow all around. The local pack didn't turn up so our boys couldn't scrummage. Selector 'Stack' Stevens and chairman Derek Morgan were pressed into service – that's definitely no preparation for an international scrum before a Test. It was blowing a gale and our handling in the backs was less than inspired; there was nothing snappy about the session at all. I like to have a kick about on the Thursday and Friday before an international, but with no posts to aim at, that practice went the way of the rest; all the more frustrating because this was the opening match of England's three-year deal with Nike boots. All this led to my worst-ever goal-kicking display for England – six misses out of eight attempts. It wasn't a case of hitting the corner flag, several just drifted off, but it was one of those days in wet conditions when I didn't quite get it right. In some ways I felt a victim of my own success – I have a very good percentage ratio playing for England.

We spent some time scrambling around at the back. I don't know if 'Woodie' and Huw Davies were tying each other's bootlaces as David Johnston came through for Scotland's first try; it was difficult to work out what was going on. On a wet, slushy day, nobody put boot to ball to clear it away. The Scots' second try came when I was robbed by Jim Calder and Alan Tomes drove through. As the ball came out, Les Cusworth didn't come for his man and our defence all came in one as a result. John Rutherford picked the ball off his toes beautifully, drew his man and Euan Kennedy had a clear run to the line. Rutherford is one of the best all-round fly-halves I've come across; he should have been the Lions' Test fly-half in New Zealand because he is a more complete pivot than Ollie Campbell.

My wife Lesley had had enough 20 minutes before the end of the match and left her seat to spend the final quarter pacing up and down behind the stand. When you have a bad day like that – individually and collectively – the media are going to make a meal of it. The knives were out after that 18-6 defeat. The 'bloody heroes' of the New Zealand game had miraculously become simply 'bloody useless'. My head was certainly on the block and once again the 'Hare Out' campaign gathered momentum.

One of the cruel facts of life in the Five Nations Championship is that you live from fortnight to fortnight. If you have a bad game, no matter that you might have played your best season of rugby, the selectors go away and in a couple of days, you may be out. It was obvious that a lot of the forwards were short of match practice and fitness in that Scotland game. Several had problems with injury and the weather had limited appearances anyway; but that only partly explains the eclipse of a unit that was the All Blacks' superior only a couple of months earlier. Perhaps they began to wonder if the New Zealanders were really second-string after all.

After the Murrayfield upset, the selectors delayed naming the team for the Ireland game at Twickenham. I'd been a favourite scapegoat in the past, and had Budge Rogers still been chairman of the selectors, I wouldn't have waited for the outcome – I'd simply have made myself available for the Tigers that weekend. 'Brace' spoke up in my defence and to be honest I didn't feel as though I should be made to carry the can. Finally the selectors retained the man who'd just become England's most-capped full-back. But Mike Slemen was out; his replacement was a young RAF pilot who'd been showing his paces for us at Leicester, Rory Underwood. Huw Davies was missing, but through injury; the talk was that Huw had been moved to fly-half at Les Cusworth's expense with Bryan Barley making his debut in the centre. Between choosing the team and announcing it, Huw's injury became known and Les was in the side. Whether the gossip was true or not, Les was determined to burst out of his international strait-jacket against the Irish. Just before the team announcement his father died after a long fight against cancer. Les still turned out for us at Newport; he, too, had come under a lot of criticism for his Murrayfield performance and

England's only win in the 1984 Championship was against Ireland; just as well because I missed this simple penalty chance with the new South Stand an impressive backdrop.

29

was fed up with the never-ending probing into why he couldn't repeat his Leicester form with England.

Dick laid it on the line before the Ireland game that for many this would be the final chance. The backs decided that we were going to run the ball as much as possible; yet, despite continually crossing the gain-line, our try tally remained at zero. We just couldn't finish the moves off. Rory had one or two opportunities, but the newness of the international arena inhibited him. Had he had a couple of games under his belt it might have been different; when a chance came against France, Rory was over like a shot. That showed that the selectors were right to pick him instead of Mark Bailey, although Bailey had probably been ahead after the trial. We lacked the confidence to finish moves off; had we done that it might have helped the forwards as well. Our winning margin should have been 20 points against Ireland, not a slender 12-9 success, and would have made it look a worthwhile win.

Because I play so far from the forwards, it's difficult to comment on the intricacies of that most secret of societies, and they all tell you something different anyway. All I know is that through the 1984 Championship they did not perform to the standard required. The line-out got worse and worse, to such an extent that when we played Wales at the end of the season the crowd cheered when we won a ball during the second half; that's something I've never encountered before in international rugby. Perhaps the biggest enigma and failure was giant lock Maurice Colclough, a British Lion in 1980 and 1983. His heart was in the right place in wanting to do well, but he spent an awful lot of time talking towards the end – and much of it didn't make sense. He had to cope with a lot of injury problems in the latter half of his career – which contributed to his international retirement after this season – but he liked listening to himself far too much. Talking is not an attribute I admire in forwards – I like to see them getting on with the job. Men like Tony Neary, Roger Uttley, Fran Cotton; now there's a breed of forwards who were out on their own when we won the Grand Slam in 1980. The trouble was they only really came together for that one season – this for me was one of the great tragedies of English rugby in recent times.

We could have done with them in 1984. The first half of the Paris game saw us soak up a lot of French pressure and then shock our opponents just after the interval when Rory Underwood showed tremendous opportunism in scoring his first England try. The essential thing to do then was to hold on to that lead and try to panic the French. Unfortunately, Jean-Pierre Rives' side had other ideas and they bounced straight back with a try in the corner after a mix-up which also involved Rory. He was learning the hard way how quickly joy can turn to sorrow in the rugby arena. That was the end for us; by the finish the contest resembled the Christians being thrown to the lions, with the crowd chanting in delight as the French gave us a good drubbing. Luckily, we made the score slightly more respectable with an excellent try on the whistle, when the England full-back stepped inside Serge Blanco's despairing tackle. Well, that's how it looked to me. It was my second international try. There was more to celebrate: my 14 points took my career total past 5,000 as well as beyond the 200-mark for England in major internationals.

Now, however, England were in real trouble, with the finger being pointed at the forwards and half-backs. Yet there was little pressure on the established members of the pack because there were no obvious replacements about. As for the scrum-half and fly-half spot, Richard Hill's injury allowed Nick Youngs a reprieve and the selectors were not going to choose Stuart Barnes because he was unavailable for the South African tour. Even then the powers that be managed to shock us with new caps for Wasps flanker Andy Dun and prop Paul Rendall, a move all the more remarkable because Wasps had lost to Bath in the John Player Cup the day before the team was announced. For once Leicester had only a passing interest in the competition as we went out in the third round to our Midlands rivals Coventry.

Many of England's problems stemmed from a lack of control from the pack and half-backs. We just weren't organised as a unit on the field in the Championship, although the team was sorted out a bit in South Africa with 'Scottie' as captain. To me all those press-ups plus running on the mornings after internationals were a joke. International players have a good Saturday night and you go training at your club on a Monday to get rid of your weekend excesses; at home matches you've got your wife with you, so you don't want to leave her on her own on a Sunday morning. The Five Nations

31

Championship is very time-consuming. You can be away from Wednesday night until Sunday. Then there's Monday training at Stourbridge – to get there I used to have to leave in the middle of the afternoon for a three-hour drive, which meant getting home around one in the morning. And Tuesday is market day, so that meant the dawn patrol again. The only plus mark for Stourbridge was the meal afterwards. All in all, you could be away for five or six days every fortnight during the Championship.

I couldn't comment on Paul Rendall's selection for the Wales game because, as I've already stated, the front row is a closed book to most backs, and certainly to full-backs. But as far as John Hall was concerned, I could not see why he had been discarded. I couldn't really work out the selectors' thinking at this stage, nor what they were trying to achieve. John Hall had come on against Scotland when Paul Simpson was injured and kept his place for the next two games. He looked the part, both in build and performance; I imagined the blindside was going to be his own for years to come. But out he went for the Wales game, and his remarkable displays afterwards in South Africa made the decision even harder to understand.

We failed to beat Wales at Twickenham for the first time since 1978, although I managed five penalties out of five. Again we failed to score a try. The Welsh were not that impressive. What was most depressing about the Championship last season was the general standard. It was certainly one of the worst Championships I've ever played in. I'm not knocking Scotland's feat of collecting only their second Grand Slam because it takes a good side to win all four matches, whatever the standard of the rugby. Yet we didn't make it easy for Scotland and had I kicked a normal quota of penalties, who knows.

A Year in the Life: The Worst is Yet to Come
In the players' minds it was never an absolute certainty during the year that the South African tour would be on. We knew the administration would want to go, but we felt the government might well step in to stop it; looking back, that might not have been such a bad idea. A lot of players were unavailable for a variety of reasons, but it was time – or should have been – for England to look at some others to try to bring back some success in the Five Nations; the squad that

had served over the previous two years had not done too well (eight games, one win and a grand total of three tries).

Several of those players – who may have appeared to have been chosen in place of others who were not available – would have gone anyway; of course, there were one or two exceptions, but overall the squad needed a change. Unfortunately, South Africa is not really the ideal place to go for changes! We picked the best team in the circumstances. To some people selecting John Fidler might have seemed a step backwards, but there must be some experience in the second row and it was up to the newcomer, Dave Cusani, to prove himself on the tour and push the seasoned campaigner out of the Test team. The injury to Jim Syddall was highlighted as a big loss, but with John Scott picked as captain and as the front jumper, what would the selectors have done had he been fit? Jim is good enough to jump at the front for England, but then where would they have played 'Scottie'? The selectors obviously felt that his No. 8 capabilities weren't there any more.

As regards behind the pack, we kept hearing about all these young up-and-coming scrum-halves we had in England. Everyone said that Nigel Melville was the man, but at the time he had yet to pull on an England jersey in an international, so we hadn't seen that great potential realised. It always seemed that whoever played for England in the number 9 shirt was not as good as Nigel Melville. To me, a player is only as good as he is when he has performed for England. It's the same when the cricketers were in trouble with the West Indies and people wailed: 'if only Graham Gooch or Peter Willey were available . . .' Anyone who didn't play rugby for England last season seemed to be a bloody good player. The critics used to say that Paul Dodge was an ordinary centre; then he broke a leg and suddenly, without playing, he had become a world-beater. The media are quick to latch on to certain comments made by administrators about the future saviours of English rugby.

England's most successful club and county had made little con- tribution to the national side during the year, despite the contest between Bath and Bristol in the John Player final and Gloucester- shire's defeat of Somerset in the Thorn EMI final. I don't play in the county championship any more, but it's not difficult to see why Gloucestershire are so successful; anyone who can't pick a good team from the best of Bristol and Gloucester needs his head examining. Those two clubs play the toughest rugby around by meeting lots of Welsh clubs. I would back Gloucestershire to do well every year. The diehards point to their continuing success as an excuse for retaining the county championship – that's not relevant. I know their administrators won't like it, but their place at the top is based on the hard work of those two clubs during the whole season, not by the county in five or six matches.

A couple of weeks before the South African party was announced Peter Wheeler declared that he would not be going for business and personal reasons. The word went out that 'Brace' had been given the nod by the selectors that he wouldn't be required for duty. But knowing him as I do I think he had half made up his mind before the need arose for any safe decisions. Pete had had a long season at the end of his career and the pressures of leading an England team that hadn't done too well were a little too much for him, compounded as they were by the commitments of business and home life. Peter knew that he was reaching the end of the international road, and that he was having a job to cope in the front row, although his experience more than compensated for this.

We had our own problems at Leicester when the local council, who hold the lease on Welford Road, threatened to impose sanctions if any Tigers went on the tour. That was no great surprise – I've frequently seen how petty people can be. I asked those same people if they'd been to South Africa and seen the situation for themselves. Of course, it was a rhetorical question. South Africa is a long way from being perfect, but we played coloured and black sides, then a mixture with whites in representative teams. So Rugby Union was not doing them an injustice. How strange it is that some hope to end the segregation in South Africa by discriminating against sportsmen. If a big business was going bust in Leicester and the only lifeline was a contract with South Africa, they would take it. In the end, only three Leicester men made the trip – Nick Youngs, Paul Dodge and myself; 'Brace' was unavailable, as were 'Woodie', Steve Redfern and Rory Underwood. Les Cusworth was not picked after deciding to put his teaching job on the line to go.

Twickenham didn't help matters by treating the whole tour as an undercover exercise: it seemed as if we were back in 1944 with the secrecy which surrounded D-Day as everyone wondered what day we were going to leave and which beach we were going to hit. The Union had made the decision to go; obviously, we were going to have to face some flak so why not be open from the word go? Having made their choice, the authorities left themselves open to even more criticism by behaving as though there was something to hide. If you had asked the people in the street how much they cared about us going, nine out of ten probably wouldn't have been bothered one way or the other. The hush-hush continued as our whereabouts in London before departing were kept quiet. One of the lighter moments came when the squad was being kitted out. The tour manager, Ron Jacobs, also the president of the RFU, was being fitted for his trousers. Ron, nicknamed 'the Badger', looks as though he has spent most of his life on a horse. Huw Davies is never slow to miss an opportunity and inquired: 'Ron, when they take your inside leg do they go straight to the ground or follow your leg all the way round?'.

Ron was part of a dual management with the chairman of selectors, Derek Morgan, as team manager. It sounded reasonable enough for Ron to do all the talking and take all the flak, leaving Derek to get on with looking after us, but in the event it was an obvious case of overmanning with the pair falling over each other during the trip, leaving Derek as a spare part for much of the time. We ended up with more chiefs than indians: by the second Test it seemed as if half the committee were there. When we needed them in America, a newish rugby country crying out for help, there was hardly anyone there to fly the flag for rugby.

Our itinerary wasn't designed to do us any favours. Seven games were scheduled, but only three were of any importance; unfortunately two of those were the Tests. That was ridiculous; on a short tour we should have played just one international with one or two more provincial teams on the list.

It was a big blow to the party when John Carleton found he was unable to go. J.C. is one of the best right wingers in the world and had distinguished himself in a fairly undistinguished side, so his loss was keenly felt, although both Tony Swift and David Trick had appeared in the 1983 Championship – on the left wing. Mark Bailey came in as Rory Underwood was required for RAF duties and

BOB THOMAS

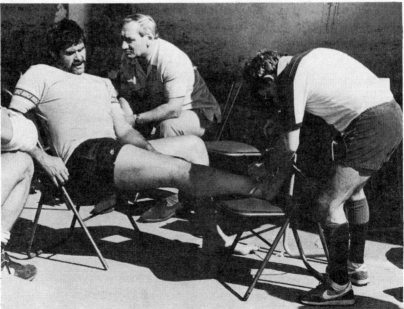

Above: *Rugby Union president and tour manager Ron Jacobs (left) did most of the talking in South Africa; team manager Derek Morgan, as ever, standing by.*
Below: *John Fidler, lock, Gloucester and England, 'Gentlemen, we have the technology to rebuild him . . .'*

'Dodgy' was back from injury. Bryan Barley was an original choice in the midfield, but dropped out allowing John Palmer a place. John had been on the fringe for several seasons so, although uncapped, the Bath centre was fairly experienced. The final member of the midfield trio was Steve Burnhill from Loughborough University, a relative unknown who had played well for the Students. That last spot was always going to go to a youngster and for a time the Cambridge Blue Kevin Simms looked a likely choice. Still, Burnhill went out there without ever having played in competitive club rugby or having had to perform under real pressure. He had learned a lot by the end of the tour, but he was definitely a novice at the start and I could not understand Derek Morgan considering him as a potential Test candidate. The selectors had given themselves another option by picking Huw Davies as one of the fly-halves – several of his England caps had been in the centre. John Horton was recalled to the other spot. Stuart Barnes had exams, and the selectors finally decided that Les Cusworth wasn't up to international standard. That must have been a difficult decision because Les is a very good fly-half when he can dictate matters; unfortunately in the international arena he couldn't find the time which would allow him to control the game and struggled accordingly. Some critics made a lot of the fact that he wasn't a great tactical kicker, but that wasn't so, as he has shown many times for Leicester. But Les didn't quite manage to find – at Twickenham, Parc des Princes, Murrayfield, or the National Stadium – that freedom which he needed to be at his most effective. It would be nice to play international rugby the Leicester way, but painful experience had taught us that this isn't possible. The return of John Horton was right; it meant he could fight it out with Huw for the Test place. You can't expect untried youngsters to go out there and do a job alone; you need a few old hands who can try to hold the side together with their experience.

The scrum-half spot was going to be won by a keen duel between Nick Youngs and Richard Hill. Nick was the man in possession, but his season never again reached the heights of those successes against the All Blacks, mainly because he was not given that same freedom or platform again. Richard Hill had come a long way in one full season of senior rugby and would probably have played against Wales, but for injury. The tenacious Hill won the Test place, not

37

least because Nick made a disastrous start to the tour at Stellenbosch. By the time he recaptured his form, it was too late.

The selectors might not have been too happy with John Scott as a No. 8, but he was their only alternative as captain. There had been talk that a skipper might be brought in from outside the team – Mike Rafter or David Cooke were suggested – but what was the point if he could not hold down a Test place? Mike had a lot of experience and had done well for us in Argentina, but the skipper had to be a recognised member of the team. Some of us had experienced a tour the previous summer when the skipper – Ciaran Fitzgerald – was not the top player in his position. On a major tour you need a skipper who's going to rally the lads round and keep things ticking over, on and off the field. The selection of Gary Rees might have been a surprise to some, especially at David Cooke's expense, but not to us in the Midlands; we had no doubt that he could do to the Springboks what he had done to the All Blacks. Peter Winterbottom was the only member of the back row assured of a place.

Nick Jeavons was still injured and in his absence three blindsides – Paul Simpson, John Hall and Andy Dun – had been tried, the first two had also been rejected through the season. Dun had exams and the selectors' choices were John Hall and Mike Teague. That was bad luck on Simpson, who'd responded with a thrilling display as Bath took the John Player Cup. Chris Butcher was the untried choice at No. 8. Chris is a talented footballer but lacks discipline, which I feel is what London rugby does to a player; we always seem to get a full quota of penalties against London teams because they are careless. In the North, those chances come few and far between because the players are used to hard competitive rugby and don't give much away for nothing. Scott and Fidler were the first-choice locks and the Orrell youngster Dave Cusani was given an opportunity to press his claims. The four props – Malcolm Preedy, Phil Blakeway, Gary Pearce and Paul Rendall – were the obvious choices. Hooker Steve Mills had been Peter Wheeler's understudy for several seasons and was obviously senior to newcomer Steve Brain; another name unfamiliar in international terms, but we knew him in the Midlands as a talented, fiery hooker. He hadn't been on the bench for the Midlands against the All Blacks because he'd been sent off earlier in the season for Coventry. Steve is a fairly physical character and we were going to need a few of those in South Africa.

Particular day-to-day details of the trip appear in my South African diary later in this book, but generally it was one of the best trips I've ever been on. The lads mixed well and there was no animosity within the party. Everyone got a game in the first two matches. Both those games brought us into contact with Errol Tobias. For me, this veteran coloured fly-half was at his most impressive in the Federation match at Stellenbosch; those coloured threequarters were especially tricky, far more inventive than the much-lauded Western Province back line, who were so straight-forward it was unbelievable. The real difference in the Tests was Danie Gerber, an outstanding rugby talent who was impossible to contain – he could see openings almost before they appeared, which is the sign of a great player. Although we were well beaten in the Tests, it didn't feel like it during the matches themselves. We were definitely a poor second on the pitch, but we weren't pressed as much as we would be in a home international. All their scores came from far out, which is a rarity in the Five Nations Championship.

We beat the Currie Cup 'B' XV reasonably easily, despite being behind, although we let in three tries, highlighting a problem that was to be with us throughout the trip. Nick Stringer was full-back in that game and I made my start at Stellenbosch. It was so hot – sweat kept running into my eyes, we didn't get it together at all and several of us looked rather out of touch. It started to go wrong when Nick Youngs knocked on a simple scoring pass from Huw Davies who had made a 50-yard run right at the start. We went from bad to worse, only winning in the final minutes when I found my kicking touch – at last. We had really struggled in that heat, but now the selectors had had a chance to look at everyone.

We lost Paul Dodge through injury during that Federation game, sadly, as it was to prove, for the whole tour. The preliminaries were over as we prepared for our first 'test' – against Currie Cup champions Western Province. There was little time for any experi-mentation as we got ready for the internationals. The selectors went straight to the team that they wanted for the 'test'. And we did play well against their champions. Everyone knew what they were sup-posed to be doing – and did it; one of the few times that has happened for England in recent years. We got enough ball to do what we wanted. A week later we knew what we wanted to do against South Africa, but unfortunately for most of the time the ball was missing! The wet conditions in Cape Town suited us, and the Western Province backs did nothing to suggest any imaginative moves that might dent our defence. We felt we could tackle them all day the way they were playing. Our defence was superb; our opponents never looked like scoring a try. But they stole a draw at the death. The referee had waved on a charge by David Trick on Carel du Plessis after seeing perfectly well what had happened, but he went over to the touch-judge – a Mr Freek Burger – and awarded a penalty to Western Province, who levelled the scores at 15-15.

The atmosphere in the team really changed after that as suddenly people started to give us a chance at last, and to be fair we hadn't really played well at all up until then. One or two of the younger players were probably fooled by this and thought that the Test was not going to be as tough as everyone had been telling them. But we let the Springboks get away in that first Test; then after clawing our way back, a couple of basic errors left them conclusive winners. Our build-up wasn't ideal. For a start we waited until halfway through the Thursday session before announcing the Test team. That made Wednesday training a complete waste of time. International rugby is about organisation as much as anything else – the reason why club pairing and partnerships do well is that the players are used to each other's habits week-in week-out. Leicester became successful through such an understanding. We all play in a similar of style so those coming in know roughly what sort of job they have to do and are familiar with the moves. There was no apparent reason, anyway, for the delay in announcing the team for the first Test because the squad that did so well against Western Province was eventually chosen en bloc. We could not understand why we had been kept hanging around, wasting valuable time. The game between Western Province and the first international was the SA Rugby Association fixture. After looking capable of running up a cricket score, the lads let themselves down badly by giving the initiative away which resulted in an unsatisfactory performance.

That delayed Test team wasn't the only problem in Port Elizabeth; the Thursday and Friday were public holidays, so there was a 'big match' atmosphere 48 hours before the kick-off. We had our own team-room, but outside that we were constantly molested by arrogant Afrikaners, not the most polite rugby supporters I've ever come across. It wasn't like preparing for a match at home. In Port Elizabeth, the hotel was next to the beach, with the surf rolling in and the sun beating down – we had to ignore all that and mentally switch on to rugby. In the Five Nations Championship, the team is usually in a hotel out of the way and is left to its own devices without constant interruptions and noise.

The South Africans ran away with the match only in the final quarter of an hour, but we were always struggling to keep in touch. I got the feeling that we were rather too relaxed and had been caught on the hop. The Springboks were hungry for victory, just as we had been against Western Province – sadly, we'd lost our appetite in the intervening week. The neutral referee Monsieur Hourquet gave some strange decisions against us, allowing the Springboks to live offside and steal or disrupt our possession. When you are under pressure like we were, then you need the South Africans to be strictly policed. But as Chalkie White always said: 'He's the only one you've got, so that's it'.

The boys were pretty down that Saturday and the mood wasn't helped by a hotel jammed full with drunken, baying South Africans. We were jostled as we climbed the stairs, but the lads decided not to get involved. There was no point in going into the hotel's Oyster Bar; both the bar and its occupants were swilling in beer. This was obviously the place for fun and games later on and we didn't want any part of it. Most of us wandered into the restaurant and discussed the events of the day. Afterwards, according to the Afrikaans paper *Rapport* the following Sunday, we took our revenge on the team-room by smashing it up. Our management knew about some glasses being broken when Chris Butcher sat on a table which collapsed and went over with him and the glasses, but as the hotel management were there at the time, the subsequent 'scandal' surprised us all. The hotel manager was spurred into action because one of the members of the accompanying British Press had lost his laundry and was seeking compensation.

The South African Press were something else and our own lot weren't far behind. One of the South African 'sports' journalists

41

actually wandered on to the training field in Cape Town to interview me. This was obviously going to be an in-depth sports feature because, after opening with the customary inquiry about what I thought of his 'wonderful' country, his second question was: 'And how do you find our South African girls?' I said 'I don't, I'm a happily married man' and pointed him in the direction of some of our bachelors. The South Africans seemed obsessed with the traditional and rather dated idea of a touring team sweeping all the host country's women off their feet in a bid to win a rugby series. Even South African rugby supremo Dr Danie Craven suggested at a cocktail party at the Board's headquarters at Newlands that if the Springboks didn't get us, South Africa's 'fifth column' – their women – would. He needn't have worried – their rugby players were enough of a handful for us!

But details of press reports implying that the tour was one big party had drifted back from England, mainly from wives and girlfriends. We were described as cowboys. 'I thought you went out there to play rugby?' was their usual complaint. We had, and reports like this did us no favours. On the Sunday after the second Test, the *Sunday Express* in London carried a story saying that one player who had made his Test debut the week before had prepared by drinking 21 bottles of beer on the Friday night. The finger was pointed at Chris Butcher, but as John Scott said: 'No way, Butch falls over when he's had three beers'. It was an unnecessary slur on the young player and on the party in general. Touring is as much about meeting people as playing rugby. If we have to lock ourselves away to keep off the front pages, then it will be a sad day for rugby.

It's beginning to get out of hand now – I think some press men are starting to completely invent stories. In Johannesburg, 'Scottie' eventually told one journalist that if he didn't stop it, he would start sending home some stories of his own about the way the Press behave on tour. The argument was smoothed over and quickly forgotten, but the outburst showed that the strains were showing on both sides. Relations between the players and the media are generally very good, probably better and friendlier than in any other international sport. Now when folk ask me whether the story of 'Butch' drinking 21 bottles of beer is true, I just reply: 'I don't know – I fell over when I'd had 17!' The South African Press – like their New

Zealand counterparts – are very supportive of their team and players. The British are less so – they are far more discriminating and won't blindly follow just to boost morale. They would never say that we were going to win, if they didn't think we had a reasonable chance, for the sake of national pride. Stories in the newspapers don't bother me personally, although they do upset my family. The Press have a job to do as I have, and we have always got on as long as they haven't gone overboard. 'Scottie' said in South Africa that half the trouble was that the Press just wouldn't accept we weren't good enough – there had to be other reasons. However, if England boys are seen drunk the night before an international they deserve all the criticism they get. I roomed with 'Butch' for the final week, and there was no sound of clinking beer bottles to prevent me from getting to sleep. 'Butch' was chatting to some friends quite late one night in the hotel restaurant, and Derek Morgan suggested that it was time to go to bed, which he did with absolutely no trouble. That must have been the wildest pre-match behaviour I saw.

Drawing the discipline line is not easy. Most sportsmen hate being on ceremony and the pomp it demands, but it's part of the tradition. Generally, we dressed properly and were on time for the many functions, which is only right. Having two managers you never quite knew who to take your lead from, Ron or Derek. The trouble is that the president of the RFU is invariably out of touch with players, time-wise. Ron should have accompanied the tour as president and let Derek get on with the job as manager; there would have been no problems with Ron making the speeches, anyway. I like Ron and he talks a lot of sense, but he's one of the old school and I'm sure he finds it difficult to relate to today's players – even I'm losing touch. Ron's the type of person the players look to to change the system because he's a direct talker. But the president has little real power; he's only there for a year, and if the key people on the committee don't agree with his views they stall major decisions until that president has departed. Even when the committee instigate their own reports on the state of the game – such as the Mallaby and Burgess documents – they refuse to act on these because they inevitably challenge the established order. More about that later.

The final week in South Africa was tough going and was not helped by our display in the mid-week game against a Country XV at Sasolberg. Again this showed the folly of not playing enough hard rugby on the trip, or even back home for that matter. If a player didn't make the England Test team in South Africa, he probably had to make do with three games, not one of which represented any reasonable or respectable standard. How players were supposed to launch themselves from that into the top side was beyond me.

The selectors learned little about those mid-week players. Of course, this was a political tour and concessions had to be made, but the gulf between the final three Saturday games and the others was enormous. Losing to provincial sides doesn't matter if it helps you prepare for the Test. When England beat the 1973 All Blacks in Auckland, all three provincial games had seen the tourists finish second. The entire Gloucester front row bowed out for the second Test, being replaced by Paul Rendall, Steve Brain and Gary Pearce. There was talk of a personality clash between 'Scottie' and Phil Blakeway, but I'm sure if they'd thought Phil was able to do his job, he would have been selected. To many the dropping of Steve Mills must have been a surprise. After being in Wheeler's shadow for so long, he looked sure of the number one spot. He had been outstanding in his three internationals, in Argentina in 1981 and against Wales two years later. But he was battling then; unfortunately in South Africa he gave the impression that the fight had already been won. That gave Steve Brain the opening he'd worked for and so the Coventry hooker capped an amazing year with his international debut.

The changes made little difference because England tumbled to their worst-ever defeat. We showed character in fighting back after the interval, but the match was a lost cause by then. Danie Gerber was extraordinary – I don't think there's another centre in the world who could have done what he did that day. We've been under so much pressure at the back for England in the past two years. Winger Mark Bailey was wondering what had hit him – and it wasn't only Gerber. A lot of England's trouble stems from the fact that the cupboard is bare at present, and the senior players are not having to fight for their places. The problem then is that the selectors often start making changes for the sake of it. In South Africa, the management said they were pleased with the loose forwards and Richard Hill, but little else. It's almost impossible for backs to show anything without the ball and having to defend all the time. When you're on the poor end of a 70-30 possession ratio, it's hard to play because you are constantly under pressure – and players under pressure will always make mistakes. Then it all depends on how able the people around you are in clearing up the mistakes. Often in English club rugby you are allowed to get away with it. If you lapse in an encounter with Cardiff, they'll do something about it and you'll find yourself behind the try-line. If it was Saracens you'd probably get away with it because they lack that sharpness that comes with regular tough rugby. The AGM decision not to have a national merit table was a great blow. If England want success, then they will have to do something to help themselves. England should have been the first – and not the last – to organise a tough competitive set-up leading to the Five Nations Championship. The Irish and Scots, with limited resources, have organised themselves well. And Wales have the toughest club rugby in the world. When our selectors go to watch a game they are lucky to see three players that might interest them; if the top clubs were involved together that number could be doubled or trebled.

As far as the South Africans were concerned, our tour was a great success; they were desperate to get back on the international circuit. They treated us well and our management were careful in making sure the hospitality was not too lavish. They have so much money; and, quite rightly, the player in South Africa is held in higher regard than he is in England. There wasn't much hospitality on the field; but then, before we left Heathrow, we were told that we were not going to win a single match – which showed how much the 'informed' opinion knew about it.

England's worst-ever defeat might not have been the ideal day to bow out of international rugby – and the decision was not in fact taken until early August – but I reckoned that I'd probably enjoy watching Danie Gerber a lot better from the stand as he tore England apart again in September 1984 in the President's XV game to celebrate 75 years at Twickenham.

3
EARLY DAYS

From the very beginning I was always 'Dusty'. I arrived on a cold November night in 1952. All the water around was frozen and my father visited the hospital next day for his first view of me after playing ice hockey with the rest of the lads. Apparently, I was covered in freckles and baby fluff, as though some dust had settled on my head. His first words to my mother in my presence were: 'We'll call him Dusty'. William came from my grandfather on my father's side, while my mother's father was Henry. So William Henry Hare it was – I've never understood why Dusty wasn't incorporated officially. The nickname could easily have fallen by the wayside in my early years, but it didn't, and I'm unlikely to lose it now. For autographs I use Dusty; for business and official documents it is W.H. Hare. I have never objected to Dusty and actually prefer it to William Henry. Some of the older folk – those that knew my grandfather as Bill – used to call me by that name.

The Hares have been farmers in the Nottinghamshire area for a few generations now. My grandfather had a farm near Upton on the other side of Newark; it was my father that moved to South Clifton. There were some cattle in the early days, but generally sheep have always formed the bulk of the farm. My grandfather had been a runner and loved his soccer. Often he took me to watch Notts County; the older brigade always supported them rather than Forest – County were the team with tradition. He was really chuffed when I captained the Newark Under-11 side; sadly he died before my later triumphs, and a month before England won the World Cup. With my father busy on the farm, most holidays were spent with my mother and her family. My father was a keen sportsman, too; in the winter a scrum-half, in the summer an opening bowler off the wrong foot. That all ended when he was bedridden with rheumatoid arthritis for eight months. The love of his life is the farm; he rallied round, had numerous operations, played some tennis and continues to fight on. Seeing him laid low like that in the early 'sixties was a real shock; I don't think I realised then how serious it was. As for my mother's sporting prowess, that was in tennis and badminton.

For me, school was basically an opportunity to excel in sport. After the 11-plus my destination was Magnus Grammar School; at last I could take up rugby. Newark rugby club were enjoying a successful period and they were always prominently featured in the local paper. My father was still keen on the game and we never missed the rugby internationals on TV. My first rugby moments were on the wing and in the centre, principally because I was one of the quickest lads in my age group. Those early years at Magnus taught me that I did not have the ideal temperament for scholastic work. Maths, geography and woodwork were my favourites, while I hated physics, biology and chemistry. Considering the way modern farming has gone, I would have been better advised to concentrate on the sciences rather than ignore them. Anyway, my final tally was four 'O' levels – my trio of favourites plus religious knowledge. I never had any ambitions to go further; I knew at 15 that I didn't enjoy the inside life or studying, and had already decided that farming would suit me perfectly. With my mother's guidance, I had become a fairly good tennis player, representing Nottinghamshire juniors on occasions, but all those dreams of Wimbledon glory were rudely shattered when, as a 14-year-old, I was beaten by 10-year-old Andrew Jarrett. He may have gone on to Davis Cup fame, but it was enough of a humiliation at that age to make me put my tennis racquet away.

Cricket was my favourite at school, although a row in my final year led to my departure from the first XI. The clash concerned my playing for the Notts Colts which I enjoyed more than playing for the school. At rugby our year did not take off until the Under-14s when a young chemistry master from Nottingham University, a prop called David Hold, took charge. In his two years with us we only lost a couple of matches and quite a few of the team went on to represent the county. The responsibility of goal-kicking rested with me even then; several of us had taken part in a trial at the start of the term and I was the most successful – I often wonder what would have happened if I'd had an off day! Originally, I was a toe-kicker,

Above left: *With my grandfather William Hare*. Above right: *Schoolboys don't come much more angelic looking than this*. Below: *The best Saturday fixture I ever made was marrying Lesley on 9 August 1975 at Sutton-on-Trent*.

but turned to the soccer style when I was about 15. I remember watching Sam Doble use that style at Newark – the only club in the area with floodlights at that time – and he seemed to have little trouble in putting them over from all parts of the field. Although I was accurate with my toe style, I couldn't hit the ball very far. Suddenly, with the soccer kick, I found I could kick double the distance. I played two seasons in the first XV at fly-half. Normally I would turn out for the school on Saturday morning and after lunch would feature in the Lincoln soccer league as a winger or striker; I continued to play football until 1975. Since then I have started to tamper with golf about half a dozen times a year, mainly for a long walk on a hot, sunny afternoon. I tend to lose concentration on the long holes. It's not too bad if you can reach the green in one shot, but by the time I have taken four or five swipes to get near the hole my mind has wandered elsewhere – a bit like the ball.

Most of my memorable moments at school were on the sporting field, playing for England at cricket and taking part in a final rugby trial. My cricketing colleagues included Graham Gooch, John Barclay and Andy Stovold, and on the rugby field I rubbed shoulders with John Horton, Tim Barnwell and Nick Joyce, with all of whom I was to come into contact in later years. After appearing for Notts' second XI in the summer of 1970, I was invited to join the ground-staff. At the time I wasn't sure about going back to school so I declined. When they found out I had decided to leave, they approached me again and I said yes. What could be better, playing rugby and working on the farm during the winter and spending my summers being paid for playing cricket. I was thrilled to be linking up with Trent Bridge. Once, with the Under-15s, our match there was rained off and I was terribly disappointed. My father was very supportive, even though the summer is our slowest time. It wasn't as if I could have gone to farming college and learned the job there; it has to be done in the market where you buy and sell sheep. That first winter I spent the time travelling around with my father getting the 'feel' of the business. I had to give the cricket a go; I knew the farm was there if I failed and, if I didn't give it a try, there would always be a question-mark over whether I could have made it or not. In the end I wasn't good enough, but at least I now know that for sure. I carried on playing for the second team when they needed me after 1975. A professional cricket life is not that exciting; I would come in and have a net if I wasn't playing, and then watch the county side; in the end I seemed to be wasting my time. At first rugby had been a diversion, a way of keeping fit in the winter. Now that pastime had become more important, not least because I had won an England cap in 1974. At school, cricket looked to be where I would achieve more, but rugby was to take over.

Newark was my first rugby home out of school, a throwback to their prominence in the local paper when I was a youngster. There had been talk of me going to Leicester even then, but at the end of my first season I moved to Nottingham, then known as Notts. I was still at fly-half, but moved to full-back where they could accommodate me better. Just out of school, I had been a replacement for the Midlands Counties East team that met the 1970 Fijians. Notts had a strong side, especially in the pack, with John Elliot and Will Dickenson in the front row. At fly-half was Nick Preston. Most of us played for the three counties – Notts, Lincs and Derbys. In my second season with Notts, I was invited to an Under-23 squad session at Bisham Abbey and the year after I played for them against the Midlands and then the Japanese; that second match was at Twickenham, and I felt I did myself some good with a couple of tries. There was plenty of talent in that team – Peter Warfield, Neil Bennett, Peter Squires, Steve Smith, Mike Rafter and Phil Blakeway, to name but a few. Suddenly I was one step away from the England team, going to Paris as a replacement to watch a 14-14 draw. Then, before I knew it, the *Daily Mail*'s rugby correspondent Terry O'Connor was on the phone, informing me that I was to make my England debut against the Welsh at Twickenham. Unfortunately, the world's number one full-back, J.P.R. Williams, missed his first game for Wales since his debut in 1969. Not that they were short of players. The first half went by in a flash; this was certainly the quickest rugby I'd ever played in. Nerves have never been a problem with me, although I wasn't too pleased to slice my first kick to touch. With Alan Old in the England side at fly-half I was not required as a goal-kicker; although that took some pressure off, I would have preferred to have been taking the shots. Still, my day was complete when England won 16-12 despite some Welsh protests about a blind Irish referee – our first victory over the principality at headquarters for 14 years. Later that season, England met France again, a special charity match for the dependents of those killed in the Paris Air Disaster. We had tried to get on that doomed Turkish Airlines DC10, but they wouldn't take a team booking. Eventually, we had come home on Pakistan Airlines. All the problems were because of a strike at Heathrow Airport. We were not told of the crash until we landed in London. Then Colonel Dennis Morgan suggested we had better ring home just to let our folks know that we were safe and sound as the early reports had stated that a rugby team was on board.

The weekend of the Wales match was special not only because it marked the beginning of my England career – on the Monday I became engaged to Lesley Rowland on her 19th birthday. Lesley was still at school when we first met; she had even been on the touch-line when I was in the school side – not to watch me, but her brother who played inside centre. Luckily for me, Lesley had got used to the side of rugby fields very early in life. As some of my mates were still at school after I had left, I was still involved socially with people from school, and Lesley and I started going out. Sport had always come first with me and I had never really bothered with girls – even now Lesley maintains that my priorities have not changed. We were married in 1975, when I was playing only part-time cricket. We had tried to get planning permission for a house in the village, but it was refused, so we moved into a farm that my father rented out, where we still live. That first summer was fairly rough; the builders were in and it was a case of making do.

The mid-seventies were decision time for me. I had got married, given up cricket and decided to concentrate on sheep farming and rugby. In 1976 I moved from Notts to Leicester. That switch caused a lot of fuss in the area and is explained in full in the next chapter. But my mind was made up during the Midlands and North match against the touring Argentinians. I realised what I was missing and what could be achieved at the highest level. Rugby life had become too easy for me at Notts; I needed a new challenge. Really, it was like starting all over again as my love and enthusiasm for rugby came back. As far as England were concerned, I got no further than the edges of selection, but Leicester more than compensated for this and I went on the Barbarian tour that year. England had settled on

51

Alastair Hignell at full-back but, despite his defensive qualities, England were not getting the points on the board and I was now gaining a reputation as a prolific points-scorer. Peter Butler had been given a couple of games, but for the 1978 Championship David Caplan was selected to make his debut in Paris.

Hignell was having injury problems and when Caplan, too, had to pull out, I received the SOS as third choice, just as I did four years later when a call came in similar circumstances for me to go out for the same game. In 1978, we lost Andy Maxwell and Peter Dixon through injury and, as we had used our two replacements, prop Robin Cowling had to play on with a badly damaged shoulder. Alan Old was again in the side, and again took the kicks. Considering our many problems, a 6-15 defeat was reasonable in the circumstances, but Hignell was back for the next game against Wales. This marked Gareth Edwards' 50th appearance for Wales and he celebrated accordingly. When Hignell dropped out just before the Calcutta Cup match in Scotland, Caplan was the replacement this time, playing in that victory and in the next match, a home success over Ireland. From 'one-cap wonder' I had taken four years to move to 'two-cap wonder'; but I hadn't given up hope. I felt I could give England the points on the board they were missing. Their goal-kicking ratio was not high, which was a source of constant irritation to their powerful scrum. Some thought at the time that I couldn't cope with pressure kicks, but I hadn't played in that many top games. The trouble is that once you are given a tag early on, that particular praise or criticism tends to remain with you for the rest of your career, however out of character it may be – often judgements are made on the evidence of one game. I had never established a rapport with any of the England coaches – John Elders, John Burgess and Peter Colston – and they were content to think of me as a stop-gap, someone to call on in case of trouble.

My kicking services, however, were needed for the England match against the All Blacks at the start of the 1978-79 season. The Midlands had run them close, but our forwards in the inter-national were hampered by some strange selections. Two tight-heads were chosen and John Scott was pushed up into the second row. We gave away a couple of silly tries in what was a rather unmemorable match. But, at last, I was kicking for my country and

About to take the ball from Geoff Evans in the special match against France after the Paris Air Disaster. Although I may have a slight resemblance to J. P. R. Williams in this photograph, the England selectors obviously didn't think so.

53

managed a penalty and a dropped goal in a 6-16 defeat. But when the 1979 Championship came along I was out on my ear again. I had been at full-back in the senior side for the final trial as we struggled to beat the Rest 17-13. Three of us failed to make it to the first international against Scotland. At least I had been capped, but Will Dickenson and John Butler were never to win a full cap. Dickenson, after his performance against the All Blacks for the Midlands, should have played in the Test against New Zealand. I was again passed over in favour of Alastair Hignell, who played the entire Championship. After drawing in the Calcutta Cup, Bill Beaumont took over from Roger Uttley as captain against Ireland. England lost in Dublin, but then beat France by a single point. The worst – not the best – came last and England were given a five-try hammering in Cardiff as the Welshmen chalked up their fourth successive Triple Crown. Even with England doing badly, there seemed no need for my services.

4

DECISION DAYS

The summer of 1984 was a torturous time for English rugby and I couldn't believe there could be any place more uncomfortable to play for one's country that in the torrid atmosphere of Ellis Park as the Springboks ran amok. A few weeks later England's cricketers were going through a similar experience around the Test grounds of this country. I'm not sure which firing line was preferable, but I often wonder whether I might have swapped one hell for another by turning my back on professional cricket in the mid-seventies.

Boot and Ball Before Bat and Ball

My natural sporting aptitude at school was for cricket, far more than rugby: the honours I received reflected that. I didn't progress from the England Under-15 cricket team to the Under-19s only because I left school at 17. I did make the England Youth team, though, after captaining the North against the South. Although I was primarily a batsman, four or five, I did bowl the occasional seamers. My connections with Nottinghamshire began with the Notts Colts, a side that played on Saturday afternoons in the county amateur league. The captain was one Brian 'Bomber' Wells, who had played for Gloucestershire and Nottinghamshire, eventually finishing up with 999 first-class wickets. 'Bomber' was a mixture of skipper, instructor, coach and motivator and the side was very much a breeding ground for future stars. When I joined the ground-staff at Trent Bridge there were about 20 players. Brian Bolus was the captain, but the star attraction at the time was one Gary Sobers. If I wasn't playing, there would be net practice in the morning and you could spend the rest of the day watching the great man in action. It didn't matter whether he was batting, bowling or fielding, the West Indian, at all times, was superb. Gary could hit the ball with amazing power; it wasn't that he was a big hitter, but his timing was perfect and he stroked the ball with effortless ease, even towards the end of his remarkable career. Even at Nottinghamshire, with his knee problems, he averaged over 40 runs an innings, one of the highest ever recorded by a Notts player in their history. Gary didn't seem too impressed by my little seamers during practice. Often he would miss a county game to give his knee a rest during the season; occasionally, I might bowl a ball that would have him playing defensively and he would say 'well bowled'. The chances were that the next delivery would disappear out of sight. As a coach, his one failing was that he thought you were as good as he was and didn't appreciate that most of us were mere mortals. Still, his presence was a great motivation for us youngsters.

Derek Randall joined the Notts staff the same day that I did. Derek has never changed. Our pre-season training was taken by an ex-Forest soccer player, John Barnwell, who went on to manage a few football clubs, including Wolves. He would always start with a long run and there was never any doubt about who would be way out in front. It was then that one of the old pros, Bob White, nicknamed Derek 'Arkle'. I was soon to learn Derek's little ways. When we played against Warwickshire seconds at Leamington Spa, playing his first game for the opposition was Alvin Kallicharran. Fortunately, we put him back in the pavilion for nought and one – I shouldn't think his wicket has been so cheaply captured since! I managed about 80 in the first innings as we ammassed a sizeable total. When I went into bat the second time we needed only 70 runs, but Derek's enthusiasm led me to be run out without even facing a ball. After wandering around on cloud nine, I was brought straight back to earth with a crash. Because of Derek's eagerness you always had to be very careful when batting with him; at least after that I knew to be on my guard. Derek has been badly treated by the England selectors over the years – we certainly have that in common. After proving one of the few successes of the tour to New Zealand and Pakistan last winter at number six, he was given one chance at three against the West Indies and then discarded yet again. Derek has a very good eye and is a brilliant fielder. Not technically a great batsman, he is a courageous fighter, full of determination. Never afraid to go for his shots, Derek likes to see the scoreboard ticking over; he's so quick between the wickets that you have to make sure he calls correctly. Cricket fans love him wherever he goes because of his refreshing attitude; the Trent Bridge crowd rightly treat him as their 'hero' and there's always a buzz when he goes in to bat.

Both the cricket and rugby went well for me early on. I was soon on the bench for an England Under-23 rugby match at Cumberland when Peter Butler was the full-back, and then I played against Japan and won a full cap against Wales in March 1974. By then I had begun to realise that I didn't quite have the ability to achieve what I wanted in first-class cricket week-in and week-out. Some players develop and I might have gone on to become a county stalwart if I had stuck it out, but I was being tempted back to the farm, a way of life I really enjoyed. Cricket wasn't a well-paid profession then as Kerry Packer had not brought about his revolution. Nowadays, county men get a far fairer wage. Cricket is not only physically demanding, it's also mentally exhausting as you can't relax or lose concentration for a second. Some days I could play well, but I struggled to find any consistency, so I put it down to not being good enough. I packed in full-time cricket at the end of the summer of 1974, but I carried on part-time cricket for a few years afterwards and captained the Notts second XI. Getting married was another reason for working on the farm all year round. I wanted to stabilise the partnership with my father, which was always going to happen, it was simply a question of when. It was disappointing to realise that I hadn't the talent for top-class cricket, but the rugby honours helped to soften the blow.

Our team contained some notable characters at the time. Barry Stead, a Yorkshireman, had a heart as big as a house. Mike Harris, a dependable opener, once scored 13 hundreds in a season. Still, Notts were not a great side and usually finished up near the bottom of the table, not like the heady days at the start of the 'eighties. Despite the presence of a world-class performer like Sobers, it wasn't until he had packed up and Clive Rice had arrived from South Africa that the seeds for the current success were sown. His attitude was keener and much stronger. Derek Randall showed what a fine batsman he was and a young bowler called Phil Wilkinson, who joined at the same time as me, came through. Others, like Kevin Cooper, helped develop the side and the signing of Richard Hadlee completed the process. Although the team contained two top Test imports in Rice and Hadlee, the majority of the rest are usually home grown; at the moment there are seven Notts-born players – not bad in a county of that size. Eddie Hemmings arrived from Warwickshire, though, and being at Trent Bridge seemed to give him a new lease of life as he received England honours. Now Eddie is being pushed by the young Paul Such.

Trent Bridge had seemed content just to tick over when I first went there, but in the 'seventies they decided to get the club back on top. Derek Randall and I were part of the youth policy when Frank Woodhead was brought in as coach. I was on the cricket committee for a couple of years and still enjoy my visits to Trent Bridge. I remember one championship game against Gloucestershire in which Derek Randall and I had managed to stave off Mike Procter and Tony Brown for the last few overs of the day. I thought I had got the measure of Procter and was feeling confident as I went out to face him the following morning. Within five balls my off-stump was cartwheeling backwards as Procter demonstrated what fast bowling is really all about.

Another time we got to the final of an Under-25 competition, which was played under John Player rules, and met Hampshire. We kept hearing stories about a quickie called Andy Roberts. We said: 'nobody's that fast from 15 yards'. Anyway, after he had grabbed four wickets in the first four overs, I came in to face him. The wicket-keeper had the ball in his gloves from the first two deliveries before I had even lifted my bat. Then I faced Imran Khan down at Brighton in only his second game for the Sussex seconds after he had moved from Worcestershire. I decided to bat and by the end of the day we had reached 400-odd for six, with Imran's figures being one for nearly a 100. He was very quick, but bowled short and the ball was bouncing well clear of the wicket and batsman.

Batting four or five, I had no real preference for quickies or spinners. I have always liked the challenge of spinners – Bishan Bedi was a real artist, although I met him only in a John Player match. Most of my cricket since I left Notts has been with Collingham and I suppose I average about the mid-forties. On giving up county cricket my average was nearer 70. Now my cricket is restricted to Saturdays and an occasional Sunday. The step from club cricket to international level is far greater than it is in rugby. In

ASSOCIATED SPORTS PHOTOGRAPHERS

I enjoyed my days at Trent Bridge, but unfortunately I decided that I was never going to make the big time as far as cricket went.

the club scene, you might have to face one good bowler, so you try to keep him out and get the runs off the rest. Professional cricket is always tight at both ends. In rugby you only have to concentrate for 80 minutes at a time, whereas while batting the pressure can go on much longer – just when you've mastered one bowler, a new, fresh man appears to test you again. I was a better cricketer at school; perhaps I was a late developer on the rugby field, although I'm sure more England Schools' cricketers go on to make the senior side than schoolboy rugby players do.

It's easier to spot a good cricketer at school, not least because facts and figures play a greater part in the game and in assessing ability, giving a clear guide to a player's performance. There's a lot more selectorial influence in rugby, especially at the schools level, and it's much easier to progress by doing nothing wrong rather than by being positively good. The rugby system allows a lot of talented players to drift away from the game, and not only because they find many distractions at university. Many top schools players have only got there because one selector has pushed them to the top by manoeuvring their way through various obstacles. The early physical developers can have a great advantage in rugby and often they are discovered when everyone has matured. My ambition at school was always to score a century at Trent Bridge – that's the home of cricket for me – rather than to kick the winning penalty against Wales at Twickenham. I'm still friendly with the Notts lads and play in the mid-week matches. One of my best mates is Paul Todd, who joined the groundstaff the year after me and went on to make the grade. Now he's my captain at Collingham. We played together for Newark Under-15s and the England Youth team, which also featured Graham Gooch and Andy Stovold. He was capped as an opening bat for Nottinghamshire, but the green wickets of home were not to his fancy and he gave it up.

Back to the dilemma of whether being an England cricketer or a rugby player was the more painful in the summer of 1984. Ted Dexter said during that series that with those four West Indians bowling so fast, if the trend should continue there will be no more cricket in ten years time – he could be right. One way out might be to extend the length of the pitch to 24 yards – or even 22 metres – in accordance with Common Market regulations. I relax far more watching cricke⁺ at Trent Bridge than I ever do watching rugby. Maybe I'm too involved to be a spectator of rugby – even watching I still tend to play full-back. I can tell you how the backs have got on, but the pack is still a closed book to me on and off the field. But making sure the backs are positioned correctly for attack or defence makes it difficult to be a mere spectator. Cricket at least allows me some peace of mind.

Untying the Notts to be Trained by the Tigers

My move from Notts to Leicester after six seasons caused a ridiculous furore. Although I was the man at the centre, most of the arguments raged around me and developed particularly between Jeff Addison, Notts' fixtures secretary and secretary of Notts, Lincs and Derbys, and Chalkie White, coach of Leicester as well as chairman of the Notts, Lincs and Derbys coaching committee. Jeff is now a RFU committee man and Chalkie is the technical administrator for the South and South-West. Jeff himself had made a move from Notts to Leicester in 1959. He made statements to the effect that he didn't believe Leicester had not poached me, which was not the case. It is hardly surprising when the top players in a region congregate in one top club. If you wanted to be seen in this area and play for your country, then Leicester was the place; no matter how much I enjoyed being at Notts, nothing was going to change that fact of life. I wanted tough, hard opposition, week-in, week-out – rugby at Notts was no longer a challenge. Leicester was not going to be easy. Robin Money, a former skipper, was full-back, although he had just started work with Adidas and this was to take him North. Marcus Rose was also there, although his appearances were to be restricted by university life. Marcus had shown himself an outstanding prospect at schoolboy level. Still, I was not worried about working my way up because I knew I had the ability to be the best. Leicester never give any guarantees of a first-team place; no matter who you are, nobody goes straight to the senior side.

My decision to move was finally made when the Midlands and North defeated the Argentinians in 1976. Chalkie was the coach and his influence, plus the added attraction of playing with Tony Neary, Fran Cotton, Steve Smith and the like, made me determined to try to keep this sort of company on a regular basis. That weekend also

61

showed me the many contradictory influences that come to bear on representative sides. In a six-match trip, the Argentinians beat East Wales, Cardiff and Aberavon before losing to us, West Wales and then finally to Wales. Wales won 20-19, saved by a late Phil Bennett penalty, while West Wales edged home by two points. Ours was the only conclusive victory – 24-9 – but at the after-match dinner we had to listen to the president of the RFU, Dickie Jeeps, telling us that he would rather lose than win like that. Considering that England had lost six of their last seven matches, you would have thought the president would have been pleased to be back on the winning trail. It's interesting now to look at that side, 11 of whom played in the 1980 Grand Slam – Roger Uttley would have made it a dozen had he not been injured. The entire back line was to turn out four years later. Just think, that side was all there ready and it still took nearly another four years before they were allowed to bring England success. After the match, I talked to the England selectors and coach Peter Colston about making a move – and to Chalkie White, who, through all the years I had known him, had never suggested that I would be better off at Welford Road. The decision was mine completely. The simple truth, which many people at Notts refused to accept, was that going to Leicester would give me a better chance of adding to that solitary England cap. Notts were in their centenary season and were naturally aggrieved to lose an England international. But it was my choice, right or wrong. It will be a sad day for rugby when individuals are not allowed to go where they please.

When I was suddenly running out in front of stands full of people instead of only a couple of hundred, I realised what I had been missing all those years. However, I had no regrets about taking so long to move because I had enjoyed my time at Notts. But now I was playing the kind of rugby where you weighed up the opponents' defences, knew their strengths and weaknesses and, rather frighteningly, I was also finding out how little I knew about full-back play. After a couple of seasons with Leicester and Chalkie most of my faults had been stamped out. I had tended to hang on to the ball too long when counter-attacking and left myself stranded from support. I also concentrated on my positional play because I was being stretched to the touch-lines by higher quality fly-halves, easily able to expose an inexperienced full-back with their tactical kicking. When teams came to Notts and saw the full-back had played for England, albeit on only one occasion, they would not test me out, reckoning that there were enough weaknesses to exploit elsewhere without risking me running back at them should their kicking be astray. That meant I could get by at Notts with the minimum of effort; but no challenge meant no enjoyment, so it was time either to move or to give up.

Leicester made me very welcome; I was familiar with most of the Tigers' players. Although I had got on well with the folk at Notts, the friendships I have made at Welford Road will last a lifetime. I was fortunate to get into the first team after one game against Northampton. It took me a while longer to get into the Leicester style of play; the rugby was harder, but because I had something to look forward to every Saturday, my satisfaction increased. Lesley had not been too happy to leave Notts because she had made many friends there, but my father had always wanted me to play for Leicester. Lesley soon settled in, too, especially when Tim Barnwell and his wife Tish arrived the following year. Tim, who had won a John Player winners' medal with Coventry in 1974, soon became a favourite with the Welford Road crowd. I was deeply shocked when he was carried off during the John Player final of 1983, when I was resting before the Lions' trip, and was on the danger list with a brain tumour over the weekend. Fortunately, Tim has now made a full recovery.

Those that think Leicester have done so well because of the brilliant backs are labouring under a misapprehension. Our forwards were a formidable bunch. Robin Cowling was a hard man with whom I got on well because he was also a farmer and we talked the same language. Robin could be fairly lively with a few drinks, especially when he was back in his home territory of Gloucester. He showed immense courage at the Parc des Princes in refusing to go off with a dislocated shoulder because England had used both their replacements. John White had to play understudy to Peter Wheeler in the early days, but he was totally loyal and played his heart out despite knowing that Peter would get his place back when returning from representative duty. At most other clubs John would have been first choice. Nick Joyce was a stalwart in the second row for many seasons – we had first met in the Midlands Youth team. His partner in the second row was Nigel Gillingham, who was in the RAF, and we made many journeys together. Nigel was an excellent ball player, but could have done with being a few inches taller. Bob Rowell was the captain when I first joined. Bob wasn't the biggest of men either, but he was a real awkward customer in the line-out.

In the back row when I first arrived was Garry Adey, at No. 8, who was very workmanlike and deserved more than the two England caps he received. Jim Kempin was on the blindside, a real bone-crunching tackler whether for real or in training. On the other side was Dave Forfar, who like me used to spend most of his training evenings being shouted at by Chalkie for being lazy. Dave was another good player who was picked for England 'B', but he wasn't fit for the match and he never got another chance. Steve Johnston soon joined the loose forwards; he was very quick for the blindside, although his hands could let him down at critical times. I'm afraid I didn't enjoy my rugby when he was captain of Leicester. Steve was very much the captain, and tried to lecture us as if he was still addressing the police cadets. Steve's task was made difficult because he was following Peter Wheeler as skipper. Ian Smith, who has been the skipper for the past two years, is a typical club man who has worked his way up, having done everything right. 'Dosser' is very unlucky not to have received any honours beyond Midlands recognition; maybe he lacks that little bit of flair that attracts the selectors. I don't think I've ever known a bloke work so hard. Now Leicester are in the process of building a new scrum with the Redfern brothers, Stuart and Steve, at prop and Chris Tressler at hooker. Dean Richards and John Wells look promising loose forwards.

There have been two main scrum-halves while I've been at Leicester – Steve Kenney and Nick Youngs. Steve was a very nippy merchant, he had quick hands and could get the ball away, but he did lack strength. Bleddyn Jones was at fly-half when I arrived. A lovely man, Bleddyn is the only Welshman I've ever met who doesn't blow his own trumpet. Chalkie had him playing to the best of his ability. Paul Dodge and Brian Hall were in the centre then; it took the talented Clive Woodward to push Brian out of his spot, although he continued to serve the club well. Bob Barker and John

Duggan were on the wing in the early days, both efficient finishers; now there's Barrie Evans and Rory Underwood. The Leicester wingers see plenty of the ball and we have been fortunate in having fliers who can finish off a move in style.

Graham Willars had his work cut out to follow Chalkie White, especially midway through a season. Graham found it tough at first; sensibly he hasn't tried to imitate Chalkie, but has brought his own style to the job. He's probably fitter than most of the players. Graham is working hard to carry Leicester through a transitional period and he – and the team – are bound to suffer by comparison with their predecessors.

5

A PLACE TO CALL MY OWN

There was no reason to think that the 1979-80 season would herald a transformation of the fortunes of the national side. Since my debut against Wales in 1974, England had played 25 internationals; I had been required for two, and rather belatedly at that. At first Tony Jorden and Peter Rossborough were considered better, then Alistair Hignell, a former schools scrum-half, was looked upon as the answer to England's full-back problems. Unfortunately, he was troubled by a constant stream of injuries and Peter Butler and David Caplan were given chances. Hignell had been back in the number 15 jersey for the game which marked the end of Peter Colston's reign as coach, a 27-3 drubbing in Cardiff.

The new regime – Budge Rogers (chairman of selectors) and Mike Davis (coach) – took charge for the Far East tour in the summer of 1979. We sneaked home in the first Test against Japan: as I was dropped after that I got the impression that the incoming management didn't think any more of me than their predecessors had. The Midlands – unusually – hardly provided the ideal springboard for international recognition when they met the touring All Blacks later in the year at Welford Road. We learned the hard way just how much Jack Gleeson, the New Zealanders' Grand Slam coach of 1978, had meant to them. Just before meeting us, they heard of his premature death in New Zealand and decided to use the game as a tribute to their former coach. Most sides enjoy a purple spell for quarter of an hour, then they relax and you can get back at them. Not these New Zealanders: Graham Mourie's men didn't let up for a minute, ultimately running in five tries for a crushing victory. I still regard that as one of the greatest performances it has ever been my misfortune to see at first-hand.

Fortunately, the North of England restored English pride a fortnight later with a magnificent win at Otley. The All Blacks had never suffered like that in Britain and it was just the boost England needed a week before the international. We had a squad session at Leicester the following day, when the team was to be announced. The North had been spot on in preparation, planning, personnel and execution. Sadly, England's men in charge didn't quite see this – only seven of the North team made it to Twickenham a week later. Steve Smith was back in favour at scrum-half and John Carleton won his first cap on the right wing. The other backs were Tony Bond and Mike Slemen. The formidable trio of forwards was Bill Beaumont, Fran Cotton and Tony Neary. Yet two glaring omissions were Alan Old and Roger Uttley, who had played major roles in the North's victory. Of course, I was delighted for fly-half club colleague Les Cusworth, who was to make his debut, but it would have been a day tailor-made for Old. And by replacing Uttley with Mike Rafter the selectors sacrificed too much height and bulk in the line-out. Again, confidence sagged in the knowledge that there were better players outside the team. Furthermore, if the selectors wanted Les in the team, he should have been allowed to play a more expansive game – his normal style. But our powerful pack – not the most mobile of units – needed the ball put accurately in front of them: while Les struggled, Alan Old could have obliged with his eyes shut.

Not surprisingly, the All Blacks were let off the hook, mainly because we were short of key players to press home the psychological advantage gained for us by the North. Nevertheless, we still could have won – I bounced a penalty off the bar which would have put us 12-10 in front – instead the All Blacks hung on to their one-point lead until the end.

It was another golden opportunity thrown away. Personally, after my disappointing summer tour, I was happy just to be settled in the squad. And at least the All Blacks' defeat primed the minds of our selectors to concentrate on the Championship. Normally England trials tend to destroy aspirations if anything, but they turned up trumps this season in the formidable form of Phil Blakeway. Uttley came into the side and John Horton was recalled at fly-half. Now this was a side that could do something; as yet, though, any talk of the Grand Slam for England was premature to say the least. Our opening game, although at home, was to be against Ireland, who were everybody's favourites for the Championship. They had just returned from Australia with two Test victories, a feat which had been beyond Wales and England in previous years.

It was disappointing that Alan Old could only find a place as a replacement. The selectors were saying: 'OK, "Oldie" is getting on a bit, but he will make a good bench player'; that was not on and very unfair, although he was given the chance to play a part, and contributed as much as anyone, in our subsequent achievements. John Horton played well, though, and was familiar with his half-back partner Steve Smith. Suddenly, everything clicked as the England squad all tuned in on the same wavelength. The pack was experienced and Mike Davis was sensible enough to work alongside it in sorting out the problems. Another bonus for our first challenge was that England had a man on the inside, well at least Lancashire and the North did. Making his debut for Ireland was the Broughton Park full-back Kevin O'Brien; Kevin was a good attacking player, but Steve Smith and the rest of his Lancashire colleagues reckoned there were chinks in his defence which could be exploited.

Strangely, the All Blacks had not tried to expose Kevin at Otley, mainly because the tourists played the attacking and erratic Eddie Dunn at fly-half. With a powerful wind behind them in the first half, normally the ball would have plummeted out of the sky towards the inexperienced O'Brien and J.C. O'Brien's presence in the North team spoilt the dreams of one veteran Northern supporter who apparently rushed up to Budge Rogers after the emphatic victory and pushed the middle page of the programme under his nose, insisting: 'There's the bloody team, Rogers; now get it picked!' Even if Budge had wanted to do that, only 14 of that North side could have found their way to Twickenham, at least with England. O'Brien had now made it with Ireland, only to find no favours from his county colleagues, as 'Smithie' and John Horton teased and taunted him unmercifully.

England's cause was helped in that Ireland were not only favourites for our game, but for the title. The pressure was eased slightly, and even when that famed Ollie Campbell boot took Ireland to 9-3 midway through the first half we felt no panic, although there was no disguising a general feeling of *déjà vu*. Then our experienced and enormous scrum – Cotton, Wheeler, Blakeway, Beaumont,

Horton (in for the injured Colclough), Uttley, Scott and Neary – began to get on top, and we roared in front with two late first-half tries. One of those came when Smith's penetrating left foot caught out O'Brien, and Mike Slemen was on hand to punish the error with a try in the corner. England turned with the score 15-9 in our favour. We consolidated with a further try by John Scott, who showed his delight in his first international try with a raised fist salute, a gesture which did not impress certain members of the committee; coach Mike Davis was actually told to tell him not to do it again.

It was a special day for me: after an international career that went back six seasons, I'd actually played two consecutive games for my country; not that I allowed myself any hope of a permanent place. Nigel Horton found out that evening just how secure any member of the England team was. Nigel had been a replacement for the injured Colclough, but there had really been little to choose between the two. The understudy certainly did himself no harm with his display that day, yet Nigel knew in his heart that Maurice would be back when fit. Budge still somehow managed to upset the victory glow by telling Nigel that he would definitely not be required for the next match. It was a matter which should have been diplomatically side-stepped at the Hilton on Saturday night. Another blow had been the loss of Tony Bond with a broken leg, although this injury had given Clive Woodward the opportunity to make his international debut. 'Bondie' was a grave loss because he was one of the few centres around strong enough to punch his way back to the pack and stay on his feet long enough for Tony Neary to take the ball from him.

Mike Davis was beginning to establish a relationship with the players. The absence of Fran Cotton, Tony Neary, Roger Uttley and Steve Smith from the Far East tour had meant he had to introduce himself all over again on his return. Mike had been absent from the senior game for a long time, and his coaching reputation had been built on some spectacular successes with the England Schoolboys. Bill Beaumont, as skipper, helped Mike a lot in his relations with the team. Mike as coach knew enough to use the vast experience available, and not to try to lay down the law. But being a newcomer also meant he carried little weight initially with the rest of the selectors, who followed Budge Rogers' lead. Mike had wanted Roger Uttley for the All Blacks game, but had been outvoted when the other selectors insisted that someone with Roger's history of back trouble would be an unnecessary risk. Thankfully, the New Zealand defeat switched the balance of power in Mike's favour, and the new coach was given the side he wanted for the Championship. We had not been made over-confident by our Irish success because the next game was in Paris, where England had not won since 1964, and had suffered some horrendous defeats in the 'seventies. However, those defeats were forgotten as our forwards showed they were the dominant force in our bid for the Championship; they controlled the French throughout, even after trailing to a try by Jean-Pierre Rives right at the kick-off. Normally that set-back would have signalled the hoisting of the England jersey in surrender, but Frannie and company were going to go down fighting if necessary, as Fran demonstrated by giving away a penalty and three points, a necessary investment because it stopped French prop Paparemborde from using illegal tactics to disrupt the English scrum.

In an ideal world, players would not have to take the law into their own hands, but the front row secret society tends to deal with its own problems. Apparently, Budge Rogers wanted to highlight Frannie's outburst, but Mike saw that such histrionics would disrupt team spirit. The chairman had managed that successfully after the Irish game, but he was prevented from wrecking our celebrations a second time. It took us a fair time to relax after the victory and everyone was too exhausted to do anything in the dressing-room. The final ten minutes had been hectic as we hung on to a four-point lead, and a couple of missed touches put us under great pressure. If we hadn't been so shattered, we would have jumped for joy at the final whistle. At first, we reflected that even with all that domination up front, the French hadn't been very far behind at the finish.

Now, for the first time, we entertained serious thoughts about the Championship: two down with two to play – and a home game against the Welsh the next obstacle. But first came the night after the French match! Paris is always a great evening out – there's little to choose between the French capital, Edinburgh, Dublin and Cardiff. The worst international evening, as far as the players are concerned, is the after-match dinner in London. Everywhere else the players can sit together – it's not only Lions' tours that cement friendships with opponents and occasional team-mates. At the

Hilton we are all split up. I have often wondered how visiting players manage to cope so patiently with this ordeal. Generally, we want to relax after these tough matches, and 'heavy' rugby chats with strangers are not the perfect way to do so.

Unfortunately, there was no escaping the tension before the match with Wales. It had all the pre-fight build-up of an Ali-Frazier title clash. Such propaganda has never affected me anyway – you always feel slightly out of things at the back. I suppose I might be a different sort of character if I had inhabited the forwards' environment where there is a lot of physical punishment. The media fuelled the fire by claiming that Frannie had called Graham Price a cheat. But the man of the moment was Paul Ringer, who had been heavily criticised for his robust performance in the previous match against France. I had played with him in my Nottingham days; seldom out of the action and very strong, he had a tendency to go over the top with rough play. I have never seen a player as psyched up as Ringer was before that match. The Welsh flanker was stalking about, trying to out-stare John Horton like a prize-fighter.

I needed treatment after a thump in the back; only on TV later did I see Ringer knee me with the ball yards away. After several other flare-ups, referee David Burnett warned both captains that the next offender would go off. Almost immediately Ringer made a high challenge on Horton; for once a referee, having issued his ultimatum, was strong enough to keep his word and Ringer was ordered off. Unpleasant though that final step was, it was the only way to diffuse this explosive situation – but even this wasn't enough as the match and tempers remained at fever pitch. Roger Uttley was led off injured, but for once the English pack would not be intimidated by these opponents who had been used to physical supremacy in the 'seventies and, on the whole, our lads kept their heads despite the muddy conditions. My penalty from Ringer's charge on Horton put us ahead, but a mix-up at the back of the scrum involving 'Smithie' allowed Jeff Squire to sneak in for a try. A second penalty regained the lead, but 'Smithie' had a kick charged down by Alan Phillips in the dying minutes which led to a try by Elgan Rees. 'Dodgy' – ever aware – had raced back to stop him going under the posts, but Rees still touched down to make the conversion little more than a formality.

71

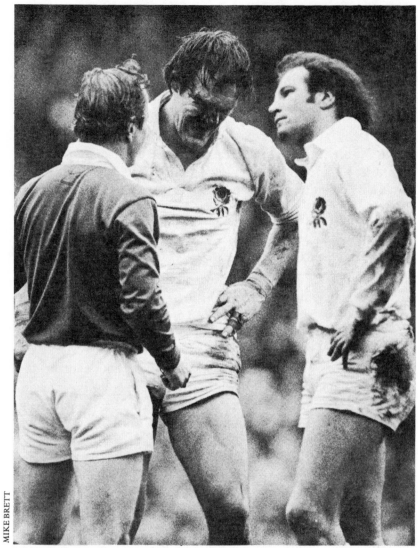

MIKE BRETT

The infamous Ringer match. Roger Uttley has come off second best in a brush with Geoff Wheel's boot and has had his classic features distorted.

Fortunately for us, Wales had spent the afternoon swapping their goalkickers around, trying Steve Fenwick, Allan Martin and Gareth Davies without success. Because of the rain, I had found my non-kicking foot was slipping, but I was able to come to terms with this during the match. Due to the changes, none of the Welsh kickers had had a chance to settle into any sort of rhythm, so their attempts had been something of a lottery. Gareth Davies was given the final responsibility. He missed, and so England were still in with a shout, two points behind, with the seconds ticking away. Suddenly we had a final penalty chance wide out on the right. The crowd were going frantic, and I realised that this kick was for the match. Really there wasn't enough time for the pressure to get to me. Anyway, goal-kicking is my job in the side. I'd come to terms with the conditions and was confident of the ground and of making the kick, which Gareth Davies hadn't been as he ran up for his conversion. Only watching it on TV later did I start to feel my stomach churn. In some ways those slim chances from the touch-line are preferable to a final opportunity from about 30 yards in front. Even the best in the world is not always expected to make it from such a wide angle. I remember when Clive Woodward was caught offside in Cardiff the following year and gave Wales a simple chance to wipe out our 19-18 advantage, Steve Fenwick took the kick so quickly that it just squirted over. That's real pressure – when there's absolutely no excuse for missing a simple chance with a Five Nations match at stake.

As my penalty kick went over, one person was even more delighted than I was – 'Smithie'. In American Football terms, the two Welsh tries had been down to his 'assists'. For once in his life, the smile was wiped off his face and Steve looked distraught when Elgan Rees scored. As I put us back in front, he rushed over and I thought he was going to give me a big kiss. I told him to get back and concentrate on keeping the Welsh out for the final two minutes. I've often wondered whether those three penalty points saved 'Smithie's' international career – anyway, he's still buying me drinks.

According to the media that weekend, the match had almost signalled the start of World War Three; yet there have been games just as dirty which haven't had a tenth of that publicity. There was no excusing the unsavoury incidents on view for millions to watch at

Twickenham that afternoon, but the violence was blown up right out of proportion. Ugly rugby or not, England were one game away from their first Grand Slam for 23 years, and we had a month to prepare for the Calcutta Cup challenge at Murrayfield. Those four weeks gave us time to relax; had it been a fortnight, the lads might still have been on edge suffering the after-effects of the Welsh match, and besides, Roger Uttley would not have recovered from his facial injury in time.

Instead, we were physically and mentally ready for the Scots, as we showed by making the game safe early on with a 16-point advantage. Andy Irvine's side played their part with some spectacular running later on, but the Scots were always going to come second. Despite the pressure, it was one of the most enjoyable games I've ever played in, but I was absolutely shattered at the finish. I always remember Frannie catching the ball near the end and hoofing it downfield into touch; he pointed to his boot and said 'That's how it's done!' It was a great day for the veteran forwards like Fran, 'Nero' and Roger, but the English hero was Clive Woodward. 'Dodgy' was back as his partner, having come into the team when Nick Preston dropped out before the game against Wales, and 'Woodie' weaved his unique magic leaving the Scottish defence in tatters, and making tries for John Carleton and Mike Slemen. That blend of old and new had carried England to the top of the table after a generation in the wilderness. My long wait was over too, but really the success belonged to the elder statesmen of the pack. Although I kicked that penalty against Wales, I still felt like one of the also-rans because there were so many much more experienced players than me. That's not to say I was some sort of an accessory, but the pressure was off because the Press had a lot more senior men to go and talk to. That was no great upset because I could watch how they handled those situations; their examples were a help to me in the years ahead.

Our celebrations in Edinburgh were mixed with discussions about the British Lions party which was being selected that weekend for the tour of South Africa. As Grand Slammers, England were going to provide the bulk of the party, although 'Nero' and Roger Uttley had made themselves unavailable. I hadn't thought I was in with much of a chance – I was still grateful to be playing for England

– how right I was! With people like Andy Irvine around, I was struggling, but when they picked Bruce Hay and Rodney McDonnell as the two full-backs I was surprised and rather upset. There was always a chance the England success might have carried me forward, but it was no great disaster to me. Others who failed to get an original call were 'Smithie', 'Dodgy' – both of whom eventually flew out as replacements – John Horton and 'Scottie'. With Ollie Campbell, Tony Ward, Gareth Davies and John Rutherford around, John Horton was always going to struggle, but John Scott was unfairly treated – as happened again three years later – because he'd been in tremendous form and had made great strides under the tutorage of 'Nero' and Roger. 'Dodgy', too, proved a point, bringing a rare poise to the Lions' back line when called for to face the Springboks. As for me, at least there were some happy memories of the previous winter to look back on and – for the first time – I had an international rugby future to consider.

6
THE WHITE LIGHT
SHINES BRIGHTEST

It has always been difficult to convey the effect Leicester Rugby Club has on those lucky enough to be involved there. The word affection fails to describe fully the players' 'love affair' with the place and its people. Our recent success and the manner in which we've stayed at the top, by the skilful blending in of new talent, is reminiscent of Liverpool's continuing soccer glory at Anfield. But our style, and the type of player we attract, are much more in keeping with Manchester United. I like to think, in rugby terms, that we have the same sort of charisma as the Old Trafford team. Even when the Tigers were not as fashionable as they have become, they still provided a temporary home for the likes of Tony O'Reilly and Ken Scotland. Like United, we have a good ground and a loyal following. Last season, after we'd been beaten at Coventry in the John Player Cup, around 7,000 people came to watch us in a friendly against Bedford on a cup Saturday.

The man who started the Leicester ball rolling was Chalkie White. Yet we would have been happy to lose him to the national side after our first cup triumph in 1979. Leicester had been in the final the year before, and Chalkie was established as one of the best club coaches in the country. Peter Colston was coming to the end of his England spell in 1979, and any thoughts of his remaining were left buried behind England's try-line in Cardiff that year as Wales romped to a 27-3 victory. Chalkie had one serious rival, Des Seabrook of Lancashire. Many of his players – Fran Cotton, Tony Neary, Bill Beaumont – were bound to be in the national squad, and Des had proved himself to be a winner at the level seen as the natural stepping-stone from club to country. Unfortunately, while the players are expected to chart this course in their bid for honours – prompted by veiled threats about failing in their duty to support the system if they don't – the powers that be have repeatedly decided to look elsewhere for the coach to guide the country's national aspirations. And that's exactly what they did in 1979. Ignoring both the most successful county coach and the most successful club coach, they plucked Mike Davis from the rugby cradle, where he was in charge of England's schoolboy teeny-bopper hopefuls. We hadn't wanted to lose Chalkie, but knew that England was a new challenge he deserved, wanted and needed. I often wondered how much England's snub spurred him into taking the Tigers to a hat-trick of John Player Cups and permanent possession of the trophy.

I used to give him a lift now and again around that time, but he never said anything about it to me; and I for one would never try to guess what Chalkie was thinking. Without him I could well have been a one-cap wonder; I owe him everything I've achieved in rugby – and a lot more. If it hadn't been for Chalkie I wouldn't have written this book, although some might see that as one of his biggest mistakes! I was surprised when he went on to become the technical administrator in the South-West; not only because he was joining the establishment, but because he hadn't gone for the Midlands job. But by then I think he had realised that he was never going to coach England, and saw an area coaching appointment as the next best thing. His familiarity with the Midlands scene, its players and officials, might have ended up as more of a hindrance than an advantage in the long term. Chalkie is highly respected throughout the Midlands, but he will forever be associated with the Tigers. That might have made working in the Midlands difficult – not because of Chalkie, but because of others less gifted and more ambitious. I'm not sure how happy he was down at Taunton early on; there's a lot more to the South-West than just Bath, Bristol and Gloucester, an attitude which he has had to try to instil in the rugby men of the region. Others may have mistaken his ways in the beginning, but knowing Chalkie, he'll stick to his guns and they'll come round to his way eventually.

After my retirement announcement, Chalkie and Don Rutherford started to do the talking, with Dick Greenwood taking a rather passive part in sessions. In recent years Chalkie has felt frustrated, and that feeling may have been responsible for one or two rather controversial and indiscreet things he has said. Chalkie had learned the hard way. When he criticises, or plans a session in a particular fashion, it's because that's the way that he has found works out of the many options he has tried himself over the years. Others haven't seemed as willing to listen and learn as he was when on his way up the coaching ladder.

There's no doubt in my mind that he would have been a good England coach. Being in charge of a regional side can be a difficult halfway house, but Chalkie was superb, especially with the North and Midlands for the Argentinian match in 1976. We knew exactly what we were to do – as individuals and as a team; everybody was organised and knew how we were going to play the game. Chalkie has often been criticised for being too intense, maybe in the same way that Jim Telfer was with the 1983 Lions. Yes, he is intense, but he can talk to you about any subject, not just rugby. His knowledge ranges from cricket to football, from local to world affairs; it's the mark of a thoughtful and wise man.

Maybe, too, Chalkie gets more emotionally involved than others, especially with his players. In many ways he brought up a whole generation of us and probably reckons that he's been in charge of some of the best in the world, as any father would regard his offsprings, and he doesn't like to see us being badly treated. But, again, I think that's part of being at Leicester. It's madness to say that because of all those years he spent at Leicester he would be unable to cut the umbilical cord, and that his rugby heritage would cloud his judgement. He would be only the England coach, not the chairman of selectors; in my experience it's the latter who's got the team he's wanted, not the coach.

Nobody's perfect – not even Chalkie. He's made mistakes in playing injured players in the past and it hasn't worked out. Now he says, given the same opportunity, 15 fit men would take the field. Again, that's not a simple choice, especially when you know the half-fit player can still do the job you want him to do. And, very occasionally, Chalkie will misread a player's reaction to his cajoling. Normally, he knows when to wade in or have a quiet word away from the rest, but sometimes the wrong approach can upset a player. Yet Chalkie is not one to hold a grudge; the argument will take its course, but once it's finished, that's the matter over with. When Leicester flew on tour to Australia, we were all pretty whacked and went straight to bed around lunch-time. But after a couple of hours' rest, it was rather an unwelcome shock to find ourselves sweating away on the training field. Our scrum-half Steve Kenney and his room-mate had overslept and arrived late. Chalkie gave them a fair ear-bashing for not making the effort to turn up on time like everybody else. Steve, normally so quiet, suddenly exploded and told our little, grey-haired coach exactly what he thought of him.

Paul Dodge is Chalkie's ideal player – on and off the field. 'Dodgy' never misses a training session, does everything properly throughout and hardly breaks into a sweat. Paul has everything that Chalkie likes to see in a rugby player; his mental attitude and approach is right, during a game he shows poise, control and a cool head. Even after a hard night's drinking when we are all making a mess of training and struggling to come to grips with the fresh air, Paul will be his usual immaculate self, if not in appearance, then certainly in performance. His loss was a major blow on England's South African tour last summer.

Chalkie had his perfect lieutenant in Peter Wheeler. The pair are fairly outspoken and had they not had such a great respect for each other, their partnership might have been an explosive combination. But by the time of Peter's second spell as captain, each had such an admiration for the other's rugby qualities that the Tigers were bound to succeed with the two of them in charge.

Some players need a longer rein than others. Chalkie encouraged Clive Woodward to go out and display his many running talents. Centres of his ability are rare, but Chalkie still taught him to use his skills in a disciplined way, how to get more out of them by varying his lines of running and approach. People were rather surprised that Chalkie was glad when Nick Youngs made the move to Leicester because his physical, foraging bursts round the scrum didn't seem to suit our style. Nick is a very talented player so Chalkie got him to do the things he was best at and Nick soon learned the Leicester way. He especially helped our back row: while Steve Kenney was sharp and cool, he couldn't force his way over the gain line with a break around the side of the scrum, whereas Nick was so strong that he could. But Nick needed Chalkie to help him, to talk to him after each game just to point out where he'd gone wrong and what he'd done well.

COLORSPORT

Chalkie White. Without him I would probably have ended up a one-cap wonder.

My contact with Chalkie goes right back to my school days when he watched me at a trial at Nottingham High School. Luckily we established a rapport straight away in the car as we gave him a lift home. Chalkie was known to me even then and I'm sure I stood to attention every time he spoke to me – I certainly took in every word! I was playing fly-half at the time and he taught me the value of using a variety of tactical kicks. Chalkie never pushed me. I was asked to join Leicester the first season I was out of school, but I was more interested in cricket; rugby was just a hobby, a way of keeping fit. After a year at Newark, I went to Nottingham where I was guaranteed a first-team spot without too much effort, even though it was at full-back. Initially, I maintained my contact with Chalkie at Notts, Lincs and Derbys, then with regional and representative teams; obviously, we had a chat every time Notts met Leicester, but he never pressured me about where I thought my rugby was taking me. Really, it wasn't until 1974 that I started to treat it seriously; and as the North and Midlands prepared for the Argentinians two seasons later I realised what I'd been missing.

Obviously, working with Chalkie in the club environment was rather different because he had more time and less talent to play with than he did when dealing with a representative side, but it's easier to set long term objectives and work on them. Although there was an asterisk after my name in the programme signifying an England cap, I felt like a novice in those early days at Leicester. I'd been a full-back for half a dozen years and there was never any suggestion of me moving to fly-half again. Chalkie trimmed up all the raw edges of my game; he stopped me running into trouble and away from support; he made sure I found touch, was positioned better and ran into the line. Chalkie also gave me confidence; he pointed out my good and bad points, then told me to go out and do the things I did well. Some coaches strip a new player down and then rebuild him; that's not Chalkie's style – he develops what's already there. He knows the players to shout at and the ones to prod gently. I was made to work hard at training – Chalkie was always bellowing at Dave Forfar in the forwards and me in the backs. There's no escape from Chalkie; his eyes cover the whole field.

Rugby was always enjoyable at Leicester. Normally it was winning rugby, too. We never had the biggest of packs and sometimes came unstuck against a set of huge forwards. Even when I arrived at Welford Road in 1976 nobody would have imagined that the Tigers were going to become England's number one club. Still, it was a pleasure to play 15-man rugby against sides happy to persist with the 10-man game. Then, with the arrival of a couple of top players, we began to blossom. Chalkie never ignored the basics; for a start the work was hard so we were always fit and could play football without flagging for the whole 80 minutes. If you're fit for the entire game, you can concentrate for all that time. Therefore your handling doesn't deteriorate and you are less likely to make mistakes. That's all part of Chalkie's strategy; he would know where to attack sides and where not to, where their weaknesses and strengths lay; how to stretch a defence and bring the ball back to leave them struggling. If it was a big game, he'd sit down with us before training and talk about it.

All good coaches have a dictatorial streak, and Chalkie was no exception. But he wasn't the one-man band that many outside Leicester thought he was. There were times when he didn't get his own way at selection meetings, which didn't please him; but overriding all was his great love for Leicester. I can't say more than that Chalkie White had the ideal credentials to coach his country – and he'd paid his dues through the system. You have to go back to John Burgess for the last England coach who really enjoyed success within the system before receiving his appointment, and he didn't last long. It must be so frustrating for someone like Chalkie to lose out to someone he didn't even know was in the race. If Des Seabrook had pipped him at the post, Chalkie would have understood because Des had come up the same hard road. But for the job to go to an outsider who had not served his apprenticeship was particularly galling. I can't think of any other sport where success with schoolboys can earn immediate promotion to the senior national team. I haven't been lucky enough to come under Des Seabrook's direction, but I am aware of the great respect the lads in the North have for him; it's the same admiration the Midlands and Leicester boys feel for Chalkie. In many ways, Des has been treated far worse than Chalkie, being deprived even of the Lancashire coaching position in 1983.

Never a Smooth Journey for the England Coach

When I first became involved with England, coaching in the backs was restricted to a run-through of the set moves. John Elders was in charge then and there was nothing like the organisation there is now. Then John Burgess took over in 1975: suddenly we were training on Sundays and showing a more serious approach to the England team. But, although I was in his squad, I never played under him. He was like the next Lancastrian to coach England, Dick Greenwood, in the matter of heart-pounding and trying to instil in us the pride of playing for England. Yet, despite success in South Africa (1972) and New Zealand (1973), England had a terrible first half of the 'seventies; there were whitewashes in 1972 and 1976, and of the 20 Championship matches in that period England only won four. Now, it's surprising England were in such a trough because the Uttleys, Nearys, Cottons and Dixons were around then, with experienced backs like Steve Smith, Alan Old, David Duckham and Peter Squires.

With Tony Neary and Fran Cotton following John Pullin as captain, England also had experienced leaders; yet somewhere it all went wrong. The biggest problem was that the selectors tended to make changes straight away, just when they had got a settled side. It was all change at the slightest set-back; quality, experienced players were thrust aside in the search for the perfect formula. I remember a great turnover of players at the time, although not great enough for me to find a way back into the team.

Peter Colston took over when Burgess decided he had had enough after the tour to Australia in 1975. Even then my face didn't fit. My only caps under him were at third choice in Paris in 1978 and against the All Blacks later the same year. Peter was rather unassertive and was dominated by Sandy Sanders, the chairman of selectors. It was Sandy who gave the team talks more often than Peter, thumping his stick on the ground and getting the lads charged up.

Mike Davis took over in 1979. Mike had taken the England schoolboys to a 'grand slam' and was to do the same with the senior side in his first season. Considering how long he had been away from the first-class scene and that he had no experience of coaching grown-ups, Mike learned very quickly. The Far East tour gave him an ideal opportunity to establish himself, despite the fact that several senior players did not make the trip. But that visit, plus the autumn tour of Graham Mourie's All Blacks, gave him the chance to find his feet before the Five Nations Championship. Overcoming initial reservations among the senior players, Mike built up a good relationship with his squad.

Mike was working with one of the best all-round packs in England's history. The decision of the senior forwards to come to terms with a serious assault on the Championship had more to do with achieving the Grand Slam than with Mike Davis's coaching, but the success was one in which everybody played their part. Our complaints about Mike early on were centred around his school-master approach. On the Far East tour, there were key words to remember: concentration and commitment. His phrases became legendary, especially his instruction to 'spread out in a bunch'. John Burgess had a good rapport with the players, but the relationship was very much 'him and us'. Mike got on very well with the players, probably too well in the end. Neary, Uttley, Cotton and the like could handle Mike's familiarity, but the younger players rather misinterpreted his friendliness, and did not always respond to this gesture of respect.

Nevertheless, until his final season Mike's record was as good as that of any England coach, if not better. After the Grand Slam we lost by two points in Cardiff, and had England beaten France in the final game they would still have shared the Championship. The following year we finished runners-up after losing by a single point to the eventual winners, Ireland. And during this time the England coach had to contend with the loss of Bill Beaumont. Sadly, Mike's last season was an unmitigated disaster and he seemed to sense that he was losing his grasp of the whole thing; it was also easy to tell there was a lot of friction between him and Budge Rogers, the chairman of selectors. Mike was very straightforward with us and we knew where we stood – with him, at least. By the end he preferred our company to that of the officials, and Twickenham are always wary of anyone with close links with the players; they seem rather scared by the prospect. This was another reason why they were worried about Chalkie White's influence, too. Both men were on the same wavelength as the players. When I was dropped after the 1981 Calcutta Cup, both Mike and Budge wrote me letters

84

explaining why. Mike's was clear, concise and told me exactly where I stood; as for Budge's I couldn't make head nor tail of it or understand why he felt the need to write. It was a strange thing for them to do anyway for an out-of-favour player. If I got a letter, everybody should have had one, but I know they didn't. So why should I have been treated any differently? Some players don't even get a phone call. By the end of the 1983 Championship, Mike had lost all his confidence, especially as he was being out-voted in the selection meetings, and signed off with the now famous 'wine into water' statement.

With the arrival of Dick Greenwood in the autumn of 1983, we felt the need to bring our school uniforms out of the closet again. Again, after a sluggish start, I got to like Dick and thought he talked a lot of sense, but he always gave the impression of over-acting, that many of his big, bold statements were made for effect. His emphasis on training should really have had little relevance for international players – it is time squandered which should be spent on team organisation, for which opportunities are limited. But given the chance, he could be fairly successful; it depends on how quickly he learns to get the best out of 15 players and prepare them for internationals; and if he's given the time. Dick fancies himself as a motivator, but I wouldn't put him in the highest class in that department. One of the best has been Chalkie White. Another was Fran Cotton when he was captain of the North and Midlands in 1976. It's more a captain's job than a coach's anyway. A coach can do it, but the captain is the one who's closest to the team; he's the one who's got to get the best out the team on the field, he's the presence they've got to react to during the game and it's his face that has to motivate them when the going gets tough.

In the same way that England's Grand Slam in 1980 was probably the worst thing to happen to Mike Davis and was a burden for the rest of his coaching life, beating New Zealand in his first game as coach has not helped Dick Greenwood. Both these coaches were raw and inexperienced when they took charge of England; suddenly they were rewarded with immediate successes, successes that had little to do with their coaching talents because they hadn't been there long enough. They inherited the ingredients of those triumphs. They had set their own high and almost impossible standards and living up to them proved far from easy. It took Mike Davis four years to turn the wine into water: as far as Dick Greenwood was concerned, he managed it in less than six months. In reality neither of them should have been in that position in the first place, especially with coaches around of the calibre of Chalkie White and Des Seabrook, who had done their apprenticeship, coached senior sides and had the respect of the leading players, and not arrived as unknown quantities. The next England coach should be someone like Alan Black, Jack Rowell, Martin Green or Dave Robinson – England's regional coaches. However, if Twickenham's past record is anything to go by then they might just as easily jump straight to a Tony Neary, Mike Rafter or Roger Uttley: all were world-class players and would be ideal choices, but only if they had learned the coaching trade the hard way. As far as Dusty Hare's ambitions in that direction are concerned, I have definitely never entertained any thoughts of coaching England . . . I was a whipping-boy for too long to put myself back in the firing line.

The Torturous Time of Jim Telfer

Jim Telfer's task as 1983 British Lions' coach was hindered by the presence of Willie John McBride as manager and the lack of a strong leader on the park. As the weeks went by, the tour seemed to be slipping away from him; games weren't going the way he wanted, the right players weren't being selected for the right job and he wasn't always getting the team he needed. Also, some senior players were opposed to his style and they weren't as easy to convince as the Scots squad were to follow the leader. The Scots lads revered Telfer and you could see why he was getting the best out of a rugby nation that had limited resources. He had brought a good unit together and given them confidence in themselves. The Scots got more out of the Lions' tour than the rest of us – six made the Test teams, while Iain Milne and Colin Deans were very unlucky not to be picked – and they played more for Telfer than the rest of us. I enjoyed his company; Telfer has a very dry sense of humour. He is even more intense than Chalkie. I would see him going off to his room in the evening with a video of our last match or an All Blacks' game and generally digesting the rugby. We would have liked to have seen him relax more, but Telfer's not that sort of guy. He doesn't drink and really there's no safety valve to release some of the pressure. I found it every alien to my normal pattern to be involved in a tour like that; an amateur in a totally professional environment. More thought should be given to how the players are treated in this situation. Telfer's main fault was that we were expected to train every day; he failed to appreciate that mental preparation is just as vital as being physically ready.

Jumping off the Bandwagon and on to the Coach!

Most of my international rugby was played in the 'eighties, during which time none of the international sides influenced the Five Nations Championship – this shows the weakness in the coaching of British rugby. I met Carwyn James only a couple of times; his early death in 1983 was a grave blow because he was the last great international coach we had produced.

New Zealand's Bryce Rope took a back seat from what I could see during the 1983 Lions' tour. There were so many senior players around that Andy Dalton, Andy Haden and Murray Mexted looked after the pack, with Stu Wilson and David Loveridge sorting out the backs. It's important that a coach appreciates that his players might be far more experienced at international or representative level than he is. This was one of Martin Green's strengths when looking after the Midlands before the meeting with the 1983 All Blacks. That victory gave him confidence and it showed in the final trial when he organised the Rest XV. Even without a training session, the understudies gave their seniors a run for their money.

The best coaching job around belongs to Don Rutherford, the technical administrator at Twickenham. Unfortunately, Don has little of the influence enjoyed by his Welsh counterparts, formerly Ray Williams and currently John Dawes. Partly, that's Don's fault because he doesn't show a lot of flair or push himself forward, but mainly it's the system. The last thing the Union expected when he was appointed was that any sort of changes would be made. I've never fully understood his brief; Don seems to spend a lot of time putting pen to paper. Being a former England full-back, he has a good understanding of back play, better than most coaches around. Recently, he had some photographs taken at Twickenham, showing how back lines stood in attack and defence. It threw up several good

BOB THOMAS

The man with the best coaching job around, Don Rutherford. Unfortunately, he has never had the backing that his Welsh counterpart Ray Williams received.

talking points, but as Don was commenting on them, he got carried away with technical detail. Basically he was right, but eventually his remarks became trivial as he brought the positional play down to a matter of inches. In some ways Twickenham have been paying only lip-service to the idea of a coaching organiser. In Wales when they felt the need for revolution, and really backed up Ray Williams and his plans for the future, the result was that golden era in the 'seventies, helped by the presence of several all-time greats. But England are still muddling along. The worst condemnation of Don Rutherford's post is that after all the years he's been there nobody really knows how good he is. And that's not his fault; he hasn't been tested to any degree. Nobody ever points to his direction or influence when England win or lose. Welsh coaches like Clive Rowlands and John Dawes always paid tribute to Ray Williams' efforts in preparing their players. After England returned from South Africa in 1984, Rutherford and Chalkie White were given a greater role in preparing the national side with Greenwood stepping back. But following the heavy Australia defeat it was decided that if the coach was going to carry the can, he should be allowed to fail by his own devices.

I have always felt that one coach is not really enough for 15 players, especially at the top level when time together is at a premium. Each season the technical administrator, regional coaches, England coach and senior players should have a meeting and work out a plan of campaign, just so that everybody knows they are heading in the same direction. Maybe then the backs might be given more consideration. In my time in international rugby backs have been treated very shoddily, often appearing to be there merely to make up the numbers, not only in training, but also with regard to the way the actual match was planned. It doesn't make it any easier to hear the constant moaning of former international backs, lamenting the so-called deterioration of flair and individual opportunism today. A quick look at the record books suggests that their memories might be playing tricks on them. Take the 1959 Championship: what an array of talent! Dickie Jeeps, Jeff Butterfield, Bev Risman, Peter Jackson and Malcolm Phillips were in the backs. They won in Dublin, drew with France and Scotland at home and lost in Cardiff. All that talent managed a grand total of nine points in four games – three penalties – and conceded 11, including one try

89

by Wales. It was just as well the television cameras hadn't arrived by then. What people forget is that they could have booted the ball off the park – there was no kicking dispensation then – and started all over again if there was nothing on. Today's threequarter is much more of a decision-maker; it's no longer a question of hoofing the ball into touch whenever you are in trouble.

Part of the trouble is that there are so few good back coaches or senior players around who are able to organise the lads outside the scrum. The man who did the job for us in the 1980 Grand Slam was Alan Old, although I would have preferred him to have directed us on the park rather than from the replacements' bench. Alan was one of the few England players who could read a game and take control. Generally, backs are far less assertive than forwards. Even at Leicester, the internationals in the back line are not dominant figures. Paul Dodge is too quiet and Clive Woodward is too individual, he has to be left to his own devices. Few seem to want to take charge. Wingers and full-backs can't – they are too far away from the action. They form a back three, as in soccer. The front five have their own jobs to do, so the real decision-makers in rugby are found in the middle five – back row and half-backs. Often that man is the scrum-half. Although I rated Steve Smith a good player, he tended to overplay the back row moves in the end. He needed a good coach to keep him in check or he got carried away. Gareth Edwards was a similar type of player who could go his own way, but the difference was that the Welsh wizard was so strong he could get away with it. And Gareth worked hard all through his career; 'Smithie' was a boy wonder, too, but left it very late before fulfilling his rugby destiny.

One of England's main troubles has been that, apart from Alan Old, nobody has directed our country's rugby ambitions from fly-half. This lack of an authoritative hand – or boot – in the number 10 jersey is not something Wales, Scotland or Ireland suffer from. Les Cusworth is a very good player at Leicester, playing the Tigers' way. When it comes to the international field, however, the fly-half has to get a grip on the game, make decisions and get the ball moving, and Les didn't manage that step. This may be because at Leicester, with the way we play, all 15 players make decisions and know what they are doing. If we come up against a problem in a club game, it's very likely not to be new and we will have discussed how

90

to solve it. With unfamiliar players and the extra pace of playing for England, there is often not enough time or team organisation to cope with problems that arise during a a game. Once again, the lack of top and regular competitive rugby leaves England struggling behind the others. Even tentative steps towards some sort of competitive club system of leagues or merit tables are resisted by those frightened of losing their power base. When Yorkshire rejected such a proposal at the 1984 AGM, it looked as if that idea would be shelved for a while, but during the following season, the RFU committee tried to resurrect it; even then the plan was for a year-long trial only. The sad thing is that the players are the last ones consulted; we are continually being told that there are other factors involved that we don't appreciate. English rugby cannot flourish while it tries to accommodate both a club and county system. There simply isn't room for both – any compromise is doomed from the start. England's history is full of the country brilliantly recovering from a crisis, only to stumble headlong into the next – rugby is no different.

7

THE GRAND SLUMP

The 1980 Grand Slam had heralded a new era for English rugby, or so we were led to believe. But with the heart of that triumph beating so passionately and effectively only because of the committed presence of veterans Fran Cotton, Roger Uttley and Tony Neary, this new era was bound to be under threat when these players bowed out of the international arena. Neither the system nor the selection had been improved in any way; England had merely followed the old method of sticking to a winning team. We had got into our winning ways only through our own devices, although the Slam was certainly a foundation to build on. Bill Beaumont was then put in charge of the 1980 Lions in South Africa. They might have failed in the Test series, but Bill proved himself a leader of rare quality – not a natural skipper, maybe, but a captain who grew in stature with every match. England's new regime of Rogers and Davis looked good because of that winning start but were soon to repeat history with errors that had cost us the New Zealand game in 1979.

Our title defence began in Cardiff and the euphoria of the previous winter left us favourites. I was lucky to be there because I'd been side-lined with an ankle injury since the end of November. Clive Woodward got all the blame for stepping offside as Brynmor Williams dummied to pass; Wales' captain Steve Fenwick kicked the penalty to give his side victory, but there was still just time for me to fail to repeat my match-winning kick of the previous year. Perhaps at that moment the writing was on the wall for England and for me. My only blemish up to that last kick had been missing the conversion of my first-ever Championship try. That final penalty was just out of easy-kicking range, too far to stroke over, and I tried to hit it too hard.

It may have been seven years since my debut against Wales, but this was my first appearance at the National Stadium. Our supporters kept harping back to that fact that it was way back in 1963 – with Rogers and Davis – that England had last won in Wales. That record always upsets the fans more than the players – I found playing Wales equally as difficult at Twickenham. Our results at head-quarters haven't been much better. Since 1960, we've been rationed to three victories – '74, '80 and '82 – which are three afternoons I will always cherish. Although there was a bit of a swirl in Cardiff, I enjoyed kicking there. But, personally, the Parc des Princes has always been my favourite, because no matter how much it rains the ground is always dry and firm underfoot. I enjoyed my one trip to Lansdowne Road, and Ollie Campbell's record there shows it's not a goal-kicker's graveyard. Murrayfield is not bad, although I wasn't at my best there in 1984 when it was really wet.

Twickenham has always been one of the hardest because of that peculiar swirling wind and the pitch is softer than the others. Luckily, as it is my home ground, I have had the chance to get used to those special problems. I always aim for the middle of the posts there, which may sound obvious, but often round-the-corner kickers aim for the right-hand post or just inside it and let the ball curve round. Some kickers get so worried about the swirl that they try to hit the ball hard and low in order to avoid the wind. I've always gone for accuracy, which probably dates back to my soccer days at school. Taking corners and free kicks accustomed me to hitting the ball to a certain man. Despite the fact that I kick soccer style, I wouldn't really describe myself as a round-the-corner merchant – which is when the kicker brings his foot round after making contact to draw the ball in – I tend to kick through the ball. Nowadays I have no preference for left or right, although commentators still describe the right as the 'wrong' side for me. The pitches on the Lions' tour were in good condition; the warm-up matches caused little damage because it was a dry winter. Rugby is on such a pedestal in South Africa that the playing areas are magnificent, and on top of this the ball travels further at altitude. On the club scene, I prefer grounds with square ends like Coventry, Leicester and Northampton, which are typical of the Midlands. And I prefer spectators behind the goal; that way the posts don't look so far away. Swansea is a strange place; at one end it's like a normal ground, but at the other there's a cricket square behind the posts.

You feel like you're kicking to matchsticks because there's nothing behind the posts with which to judge the distance. I've never kicked well at the Richmond Athletic Ground; again one end rather fades away.

That Welsh defeat was a big blow because victory in Cardiff would have meant we were effectively halfway to another Grand Slam. The situation was not irretrievable, though, and an exciting Calcutta Cup success brought us back on course. The only problem, as far as I was concerned, was when I found out I'd been dropped after that win. It was a shattering blow – the only time I had been unexpectedly hit from behind by the England selectors. Both our opening matches had been littered with mistakes, more a testimony to the pressure than any weaknesses on the part of our defence. Certainly, the crowds had got their money's-worth in the two games – 40 points on each occasion. My personal contribution added up to 30, but here I was, taking the blame for Steve Munro's try in the Scotland match. Covering across, I had come into the line to block one of Scotland's attacks, but when Jim Renwick saw us with the extra man he hoofed the ball through; it looked more in hope than anything else, but it was one of those kicks that's impossible to read as it bounced this way and that, but always out of my reach. Even now I have nightmares about it. And just when I seemed to have it under control at last, Munro was on it for the try. To most of the Twickenham crowd I must have looked hesitant, but to have committed myself early on would have been a worse course of action. It was the sort of situation which happens from time to time; you just pray that it never occurs in an international. Now it had, but at least my lapse had not cost England the game. Had that been the case, then I would have felt under threat. As a full-back you should be able to handle incidents like that, but I thought my personal contribution that season had more than compensated for the odd mistake.

In a way the circumstances of our Calcutta Cup victory hinted at my probable downfall. The winning try had come from a young Cambridge student at fly-half, Huw Davies, who'd been brought into the side for the injured John Horton. The selectors were keen to introduce young blood that season, intent on replacing the senior members of the Grand Slam side before England got out of the habit of winning again. I was next on their list as Huw's fellow student

94

Marcus Rose took my place for the trip to Dublin. Letters from both Mike Davis and Budge Rogers duly arrived, explaining the reasons why; Mike was open and plain about it and had a long chat with me at the Stourbridge session the following Monday. Budge, who had promised to talk to me, didn't show up, which didn't surprise me, and poor Mike had to carry the can on his own. He looked rather embarrassed about it, yet I had no complaints about the way he had treated me. There was no denying that I was very upset, and this rejection heralded a distinct change in my rugby life. From that point on, I decided that enjoyment was the name of the game. I would take nothing for granted, and any honours that came my way would be a bonus. If I got another chance to play for England – and I doubted that very much – I would jump at it and appreciate the opportunity, but it would no longer be a matter of life and death. My appearances for my country had already reached double figures, so at least W.H. Hare would not go down as one- or two-cap wonder, and that was important to me. And the fact that I was on the bench for the final two matches of that 1981 Championship at least meant the selectors had not discarded me completely. Mike had told me that they wanted to broaden the game in the backs. And, after a sticky start, Marcus certainly did that, bursting through for a try just before half-time and then counter-attacking from his own half to set up the winning try by Paul Dodge.

Although I wanted England to win, I had hoped the match might prove the selectors wrong as far as their judgement about full-back went. Marcus's dream debut knocked that idea firmly on the head. His try was exactly what the selectors had been looking for, from precisely the situation they said I was unlikely to score from or even get into. Budge Rogers' panel may have shown spot-on timing in this instance, but, in general, they'd come up with more minuses than plusses. The North of England had shown them the way the previous season, but they had still needed two chances before getting it right. Luckily, there had been a tour match first, or there would have been no 1980 Grand Slam for England. The need for a tactical fly-half like John Horton or Alan Old and the presence of Roger Uttley on the blindside was so obvious that to leave them out had almost bordered on criminal negligence. All they had to do was ask the players.

BOB THOMAS

Budge Rogers, the chairman of selectors, took England to the Grand Slam in his first season in charge but his behaviour undermined our chances over the next three seasons.

With the Grand Slam won, the selectors soon encountered their first real problems with the retirement of Tony Neary and Roger Uttley. Their choices were Mike Rafter, who had kept 'Nero' out of the team a few years before, and Harlequins openside David Cooke, the up-and-coming blond bombshell. It was a battle between youth and experience which the selectors solved in their own inimitable style by eventually picking both of them, almost as though they couldn't make up their minds. Cooke and Rafter combined together might have just about filled Neary's shirt, but that left the blindside wide open. Their selections made no attempt to replace Roger's immense presence and contribution in the line-out, a mistake that was quickly realised because Nick Jeavons was drafted in for the next game. Unfortunately, his great day was ruined when he stuck his finger in his eye trying to collect a pass from Bill Beaumont and had to retire early on.

The loss of that venerable forward trio – Fran Cotton limped off after quarter of an hour of the Welsh game, never to return – was a severe test of England's resources, but the emergence of Bill Beaumont as a world-class leader went some way to compensating for this departure. Bill had learned his trade well and was an inspiration to all, but suddenly, apart from Peter Wheeler, he had nobody to lean on in the scrum, metaphorically speaking. Then Bill made one of his rare mistakes, choosing to play into the wind as England faced France at Twickenham, where victory would mean a share in the Championship. France were going for a third Grand Slam and the game swung their way just before half-time when England were left exposed by a quick line-out near their line. England complained, with justification, because Marcus Rose had belted a long touch and the ball had landed in Dickie Jeeps' lap in the committee box. A quick line-out must be taken with the original ball, but although referee Alan Hosie insisted this was so, that ball was still 50 yards away in Jeeps' safe possession. It proved a crucial error because it took France clear at 16-0 and Bill's gamble had failed. England needed to take all their chances in the second half, but although Marcus was a reasonable goal-kicker, I wouldn't put him in the top bracket; as in the rest of his game, he tended to lack discipline in preparation and execution. England could only manage four penalties in reply which would have been enough but for Mr Hosie's error. As a goal-kicker I always preferred to start with the wind. That way it's easier to get into your rhythm – there's no need to hit the ball extra hard; if you lose your confidence early on then it's not always easy to get back in the groove when the conditions are right. Also, there's the chance that the skipper might have given the ball to someone else in the meantime.

Choosing and using the wind is essential in international rugby; it's not so important on the club scene, where an experienced side can close down on its opponents in the first half and then pressure them into mistakes after the interval. But international defences don't crack as easily, and you want the points on the board. In Dublin our broader approach worked because the Irish had enough problems of their own and didn't seem to know what they were doing. England picked the right team to expose them down the flanks. However, this has never been the way to beat the French; to have any hope then you must play it tight and not allow their backs to run riot. I felt very frustrated on the bench when those second half penalties went astray. France had taken our place at the top of the table, but really the bounces that had gone our way the season before had turned against us; that was all. A successive Grand Slam went begging because of a single refereeing blunder, plus Clive Woodward's half-step or my hooked penalty depending on your viewpoint.

But, at that point, there was no sign of the slide that was to take England to rock bottom in 1983 and 1984. Those that claim the writing was already on the wall are wrong; our rugby in Argentina in that summer of 1981 proved that the sound rebuilding of the squad was well underway. England have never been given enough credit for winning that series. Not only had the venerable forward trio gone, but Peter Wheeler, Maurice Colclough and Phil Blakeway could not make the trip. Mike Slemen was also unavailable and, fortunately for me, Marcus Rose had exams. Argentina were a force to be reckoned with, especially with the world-ranked Hugo Porta at fly-half spear-heading their challenge.

Budge Rogers couldn't go, so we gained Derek Morgan as tour manager and he did an excellent job in difficult circumstances. There were ten uncapped men in the party of 26, but it wasn't only the newcomers who were shocked by our accommodation when we arrived. The so-called country club was a real dive and I thought I was about to take part in my first players' strike. Our rooms at the top of the building were so damp that the sheets were actually wet and for room-mates there were an assortment of creatures, including spiders as big as Clint MacGregor's hand. And our locality meant there was no escape outside the confines of the club – not even to go for a walk. There was little we could do that first night, so we all moved downstairs to a flat. The next day we moved out.

Although I was in Argentina to enjoy my England 'bonus', I was also aware that this was a final chance to re-establish my place as England's leading full-back. With Porta around, any weaknesses in my positional play or catching would be laid bare by one of the best exponents of the tactical game in recent times. Brian Patrick was the other full-back, but I never felt threatened by him – or Porta. We drew the first Test – and won the second – and our makeshift pack put up a tremendous performance. Two deserve special mention; John Fidler won his first England caps at 32 (the decision to give us caps was a measure of our task) with the solid, workmanlike performances he had given for Gloucester and Gloucestershire for over a decade. The other was Mike Rafter who, because of his lack of size, had never been given the credit due to him. Rafter gave two of his best-ever performances in the Tests and was the main reason for Porta's relative ineffectiveness. John Scott played a heroic part, being laid low with ankle trouble, earache and literally rising from his sickbed to play in five of the seven matches. His courage and influence made a great impression on our manager.

My hopes were high, both for myself and England, on my return, but I was far from delighted to find that I was no longer even second choice to Marcus Rose. The selectors had demoted me to third with Nick Stringer moving on to the replacements' bench. After my efforts that summer I was unhappy that I now appeared to be surplus to requirements: it made me glad to be treating every trip, every honour as a bonus. If I had not, I would have been really hurt by this latest slight. Now I was on a par with coach Mike Davis; we'd both been dropped by England five times. That was not bad going in my 12-cap career which stretched back eight seasons. For the first time since March 1979 I was not directly involved in an England build-up and with two young lads above me in the ratings,

BOB THOMAS

With Steve 'I'm All Right, Jack' Smith in Argentina in 1981; a hard tour on and off the field after which I was dropped for a fifth time by the England selectors.

100

it wasn't so much that my future looked bleak as that there didn't seem to be a future for me at all.

However, after beating the Aussies, England wasted a good start to draw in Scotland and then fell to Ireland at Twickenham. Marcus Rose lost confidence and it showed in Ireland's two tries. He was not giving the team any extra width and, in defence, the young student was just not doing the right thing at the right time and was badly at fault when Ireland's Hugo MacNeill crashed through on the blind-side. Stringer was picked to make his debut in Paris – the full-back's graveyard – a fortnight later. Much to my surprise, I was brought back on to the bench and Marcus was put completely out of contention. Nick Stringer had already been capped as a replacement when Mike Slemen went off with concussion against the Wallabies, so the Wasps full-back did not take the customary Saturday off before making his debut, as a result of which he sustained a hamstring injury. His misfortune proved to be my gain, and I returned gratefully to the national side to begin my sixth England career.

But my return was overshadowed by the events which were to deprive England of their guiding light, Bill Beaumont, and create problems which were never satisfactorily resolved. The Saturday after the Calcutta Cup match, Bill had left the field during the county championship final after receiving a bang on the head. It was not the first he had suffered over the years, and as a precautionary measure he dropped out of the Irish international. Nobody could have foreseen what was to come as the selectors made temporary arrangements for a new skipper. As a one-off their choice fell on the bubbling Steve Smith, an extrovert character, just the man, they felt, to keep the seat warm for Bill Beaumont; these were the reasons they gave for ignoring Peter Wheeler yet again. Nobody begrudged 'Smithie' the job, least of all me – I was happy just to be there – but the scrum-half himself admitted that Peter should have been the man. England then completely lost their way against Ireland, running around like 'headless chickens' as their new skipper announced. Thank God Bill would be back for the Paris match. But, although he made that trip, England's most successful captain took no part in the proceedings. A warning that any further knocks on the head might lead to permanent damage was a danger signal that even this brave Lion could not ignore. Putting his body at risk in the line of England duty was one thing, but he had too much respect for the game and regard for his family to gamble unnecessarily. Budge Rogers' panel, having given Steve Smith a specific job to do for one match, thought it would be unfair and would upset team morale if another change was made to give England a third captain in as many matches. It was another error of judgement because 'Smithie' would have seen no disgrace in stepping down, and their failure to give Peter Wheeler the top job at last confirmed that the chairman of selectors was willing to put personal differences before England's welfare.

Luckily, the players have always been able to forget about such small-mindedness and get down to the job in hand, and England battled as one in the Parc des Princes that afternoon. I had been determined to enjoy what might well be my last 80 minutes of rugby for my country. So anxious was I to show the selectors how wrong they had been about me that I had spent a lot of time practising with the heavier Adidas ball. I knew that effort had paid off when I stroked over my second penalty for 40 yards. It went straight through the middle and signalled one of those days when everything was going to go right. In all I put over seven kicks which brought a total of 19 points to equal my record against Wales set a year earlier. Although it was a splendid victory I'm not sure if it warranted our victory celebrations which grabbed the headlines when prop Colin Smart was rushed to hospital after the famous 'aftershave' incident at the dinner. I felt my own celebrations were justified, though.

My successful return continued against Wales, giving us victory in our two final and hardest matches. As in 1981 the Grand Slam had been England's for the taking. This time it was lost because of Colin Smart's careless push of Iain Paxton at Murrayfield and a couple of points versus Ireland. England had lost a total of three Championship matches in three years – one by a single point, another by two and the biggest losing margin was four points in the 1981 French game. There was no doubt that the biggest blow was the loss of Bill Beaumont and it wasn't until the following season that the full effect of his departure was felt. His immediate influence had kept us on course in 1982 and the team rallied round well, but at the start of the next season we suddenly realised there was no authoritative leader about to take his place.

On the plus side, Peter Winterbottom had proved a great find. I hadn't heard much about him, but he was certainly a destructive influence on the opposition. Peter, who is known as the 'Strawman', had given Jean-Pierre Rives a tremendous clattering right at the start of the Paris match; it was just the example we needed. Commitment like that can really lift a team. Rives, the French captain, is a rugby legend, and to see him laid low by our novice blond-haired flanker was a tremendous boost.

So Steve Smith's one-off debut as captain was extended for the French trip. For me, Steve had always been better as the team spokesman, just the right sort to have as senior pro in your ranks. He's always there with the quick and witty remark, dazzling all with his teeth and repartee. When Erika Roe made her stunning appearance at half-time during the Wallaby match, Bill's team talk failed to receive maximum concentration as 'Smithie' interrupted: 'Hey Bill, there's a bird just run on with your bum on her chest'. And following Colin Smart's aftershave experience, Steve watched him throwing on some talcum powder after a post-match bath. 'Nice to see you back on the solids, Smartie!' he joked.

Peter Wheeler was the obvious choice because of his success in charge of Leicester and the Midlands, whereas 'Smithie' had never captained anyone before. Nevertheless, after our victories in the final two matches, Steve was made skipper for our tour of Canada and the USA – and that's where England's problems really began. At best it was an England 'B' trip, but the American sponsors insisted that a full-strength team go out. It would have been an ideal chance to blood some Under-23 youngsters and forwards who hadn't quite made the top grade. But for the seniors, this tour was really a waste of time – after winning both Tests against the national teams by huge margins, we came home without having faced any challenge that would have helped us prepare for the forthcoming year. Yet somehow, as the Championship approached, England was brimming with confidence and optimism. Following the tour of the States, the national side had boosted its growing ego with massive and basically pointless victories over Fiji and the Rest XV in the trial. But, in real terms, we hadn't played a proper game since meeting Wales the previous season. And, while the England XV were massacring lesser rugby beings on the field, powers were at work on the sidelines undermining the strength and spirit of the side, powers that should have been assisting, not hindering our challenge. Those who insist that England declined steadily from that 1980 Grand Slam have got it wrong; a lot of rebuilding had gone into the side since that triumph and by March 1982 Mike Davis and the players had made good progress and the prospects looked bright. Yet, a year later, the Red Rose was propping up the bottom of the Championship and only part of the blame for that could be laid at the door of the players and coach. For Mike Davis it was supposed to be a farewell season of success – and therein lies the root cause of some of England's troubles.

Mike had always said that four years was a sufficient stretch as coach and announced his intentions before the start of the 1982-83 season, primarily so that England could find a successor during the nine months ahead. But the timing of his decision brought about an immediate shift in the balance of power in the selection panel. Those who had backed him in the past now sided with Budge Rogers, the chairman who looked like being around when the new coach had been appointed and Mike had long departed. Davis's good intentions proved a gross error of judgement.

The political manoeuvring manifested itself most damagingly on the playing side in the disgusting way Mike Slemen was treated. Mike had not been available for the summer tour to the States, but there was absolutely no reason why he should have been missing when we began the Championship. His absence was a severe dent to morale, especially that of the senior players. England's most-capped wing, a footballer of proven world-class had been tossed aside without even being given the opportunity to state his case in the trial. Having been a regular since 1976, he deserved more consideration, even if that meant only a place in the Rest XV. As it was, the selectors watched four right wingers – John Carleton, Tony Swift, David Trick and Barrie Evans – at the trial. According to the selectors, 'Slem' had lost his bottle and had never properly recovered from the concussion he suffered as he stopped Brendan Moon scoring in the Wallaby match. As far as we were concerned, this was ridiculous. Mike had long been held in awe by the rest of us; he is so cool under pressure, and at one time he was even third choice full-back in the selectors' list. Maybe Mike had more chances to show his defensive skills than his attacking prowess, but the Twickenham crowd demonstrated what they thought of him by giving him an emotional standing ovation when physio Don Gatherer led him, injured, from the field in that Australian game.

Mike showed no ill-effects of that concussion when his astute rugby brain brought us nine points in Paris six weeks later. First his quick drop-out caught the French napping and he hacked the ball on for Clive Woodward's try under the posts. Later his quick throw-in led to John Scott being tackled without the ball and the resulting penalty gave us three more points. And in the following game against Wales – in which he equalled Peter Squires' record of 29 caps for an English wing – Mike set us on the road to victory with an early try in the corner, demonstrating a perfect example of how to dive through a covering tackle to score. It was his eighth try for England, two more than Squires and two less than David Duckham managed in 36 internationals – there has been no bountiful harvest for England wingers in recent times.

But the wind of change was blowing. Mike faced an unofficial trial playing for the Barbarians against Leicester in the annual Boxing Day fixture. Unfortunately for him, we were on top form – all eager to give Chalkie White the perfect send-off on his way to the South-West as technical administrator. The selectors assumed that because Barrie Evans twice left Mike flat-footed their suspicions that he had lost his nerve and his appetite for the big time had been accurate. The truth is that Barrie had had the whole field to run in and had showed Mike one way and gone the other – which is what you would expect of any good winger. Anyway, we were all psyched up for Chalkie's last game as coach, just as the All Blacks had been when paying their final tribute to Jack Gleeson against the Midlands in 1979.

Mike had been a great help to me on the international field. I was lucky to have played most of my England rugby with two such good defensive ball-catching wingers as Mike Slemen and John Carleton. We worked well as a trio with a good understanding – there was rarely confusion over calls as we all knew each other's play so well. Maybe, purely in terms of his form at that particular time, Mike wasn't as sharp as we had come to expect him to be, but in terms of upsetting the team plan, team spirit and the back trio in particular, his omission from the team was disastrous and unnecessary. He was the senior man in the backs and when he spoke the rest of us listened. Any one of those reasons was cause enough to leave well alone, even without the one final factor that made the whole situation supremely ridiculous – there was no left wing replacement around. The selectors had created a major problem where none should have existed – even by their standards the whole affair was remarkable. It was different a year later when Mike found himself under threat again, this time from Rory Underwood and Mark Bailey, who were both recognised left wingers and whose form made them real contenders. In 1983 there were no likely candidates, just right wingers desperate to get into the team. The experience must have affected Mike deeply because he'd lost his old sparkle when he was brought back the following year. Maybe he had, metaphorically, been knocked down too hard in the end and had never fully recovered.

We got the impression that it wasn't only the players that were unhappy with Mike's exclusion: Mike Davis was finding out just who his friends were on the selection panel. That decision to retire had left him without much support on crucial issues and, for the first time in four years, he was having to work without some of the best players and others he needed and wanted to win international matches. This put Mike's close relationship with the players at risk. We found it difficult to know just how many of the selectors' team deliberations were down to him. Now that the selectors had begun to act unpredictably again, the players tended to become safety-conscious and less willing to risk trying to demonstrate their capabilities on and off the field. Communication broke down to such an extent that when we were on the bus going to training in Dublin, the team didn't know who was playing on which wing. Eventually, J.C. stood his ground and David Trick made his debut on the left. Then, suddenly, John Scott having gone down with 'flu, the whole atmosphere changed when Mike asked Peter Wheeler to take over. You could feel the spirits rise and for the first time in a long time an England training session began to buzz.

But we had endured two months of turmoil before that moment occurred. As favourites, England began their Championship challenge at Twickenham against the French. Jean-Pierre Rives' men had finished bottom with Wales the season before, but had none-

106

theless managed to thump champions Ireland 22-9 in the final match, their selectors having come to their senses and brought Paparemborde, Dospital and Imbernon back into the pack. When they had played us a month earlier, their scrum had consisted of two tight-head props, a hooker and five loose forwards; Peter Wheeler, for one, although grateful, couldn't understand why the French continued to commit rugby suicide. But there were no favours from the French in 1983, and they looked prepared for a serious assault on the title. Twickenham was a favourite hunting ground of theirs. Since 1973, England's only victory there over the French had been a narrow 7-6 result in 1979. Yet, somehow, our 209 points against Canada, the USA, Fiji and the Rest XV were deemed to have tipped the scales in our favour. We soon found out how inadequate our preparation was.

The Slemen affair had not been the only hindrance in our build-up. That autumn the Adidas 'boot-money' scandal had hit the headlines and while all the other Unions promised to carry out investigations, the Twickenham hierarchy decided on a witch-hunt instead. Players were required to black out their boots and the presence of the president, J.V. Smith, checking on this in the changing-room before a match was not the ideal mental preparation for players. The whole episode just served to further distance us from the selectors and officials. Budge Rogers was very much an establishment man and his reaction to the scandal was to try to get several senior players dropped, notably Peter Wheeler. This was hardly likely to bring him any closer to Mike Davis. A squabbling management was not something that could be hidden from the players, and as we lost confidence in them, we began to doubt our own ability as a team.

We could not have been blamed for wondering about the wisdom of a panel which could drop Slemen as it did, fail to pick Wheeler as captain and then neglect to stick by the team when rumours and allegations started flying around. We had foolishly assumed that everyone was in this together – how mistaken we were. To make matters worse, J.V. Smith was exactly the wrong sort of president to have around with all this going on. Instead of playing the diplomat and trying to bring everyone together, he saw himself as the head of some magnificent crusade, fighting courageously to restore rugby's tarnished amateur image, regardless of how out of date and unrealistic that might be. I've got on with most of the presidents over the years; despite often being almost a couple of generations away from the players, they've known their place, made numerous speeches and let the committee get on with its work. Now J.V. came along and he was free to make statements every day to the Press, which because of his position gave the impression of being the official Twickenham viewpoint on the whole affair. He was also outspoken about England's proposed tour to South Africa, but the RFU have ways of dealing with presidents who don't toe the line as regards thinking their way. In the case of J.V. Smith, the decision to tour was deferred until his year in office was over. Sadly, the same methods that are used to stop a president stepping backwards can be implemented against a man of vision who wants to move forward faster than a funeral march.

This background strife was hardly the ideal springboard for our Five Nations Championship challenge. Our build-up was further disrupted at the Bisham Abbey session a week before the French match when Clive Woodward's shoulder problems led to his withdrawal from the side and Huw Davies came in. Mike Slemen's place had already gone to Tony Swift. France proved even tougher than expected; although we led 9-3 at half-time, our forwards were under tremendous pressure and any hopes of holding on vanished when Colin Smart fell across Maurice Colclough's leg and the giant lock's knee was badly damaged, keeping him out for the season. The French, for once, were well organised and stuck to their game plan. The final score, 19-15 in France's favour, might not look a heavy defeat, but the visitors had managed three tries to none. Our forwards had been under so much pressure that we were on the defensive for most of the game. The defeat was a blow, but the fact that France looked so impressive softened the impact. Until that game, the four matches we had not won in the Championship since the Grand Slam had all been against sides we should have beaten on the day; now we had come second to a better side. Yet we knew that failure would not be tolerated and that another faltering display in Cardiff might lead to a mass clear-out.

In fact, England didn't fail in Cardiff, becoming the first England team to leave the Welsh capital without losing for 20 years. Yet that

My first international try in 1981 contributed to a personal tally of 19 points – not enough to win the match.

109

result – a 13-13 draw – was hailed as a disaster and started the panic which plummeted us down to the bottom of the table. England's pack that day was left with just one member of the Grand Slam scrum – John Scott – as Peter Wheeler had joined Maurice on the injury list. England had their chances and scored a marvellous try when I made the extra man for J.C. to score, but we lost our way after dominating early on and were lucky eventually to hold on. It was not the greatest of matches and Clive Rowlands, the chairman of the Welsh selectors, summed it up when he said that the replay would be on the following Saturday, but that he would not be attending! Steve Smith had not helped by trying to close up the game later on, and his policy of bringing the back row into play seemed only to serve to allow the Welsh team back into the game. He and 'Scottie' had become obsessed with holding the ball in the back of the scrum, which slowed everything down. It had worked when Gareth Edwards and Mervyn Davies were the star players, but this English version of 'slow it down' was doing little for our back play. At the time it seemed as if the forwards were using all the good ball and finally shoving it out to us only when they no longer had any use for it or couldn't make progress themselves. Forward preoccupation and domination has played a major part in the decline of back play throughout Britain in recent times. We had not lost the match, but we might as well have done for the reaction we got – even our own selectors treated it like a defeat.

Anyway, 'Smithie' should have been warned to watch his back when Budge told him that he would deal with the press conference after the match and that it would be better for the captain to stay and look after the lads. Budge, with the skipper conveniently out of the way, then laid the blame for England's failure to win firmly on the shoulders of the half-backs, 'Smithie' and Les Cusworth. It was a cowardly way of behaving and was guaranteed to dispel our already diminishing confidence. After Budge's comments, the axe was bound to fall on those two, and it did. John Horton was brought back at fly-half, Nigel Melville was the new scrum-half and John Scott the new captain. Again Peter Wheeler had been passed over; with Budge controlling the selection panel and Mike Davis almost in exile, 'Brace' would be their last choice. John Scott had proved himself a successful captain of Cardiff, but he didn't function as

Steve Smith thought he had seen it all, but even he could not believe the way Budge Rogers betrayed him after the Wales game in 1983.

111

a skipper in building up the morale of international players. Perhaps the players weren't there to boost up, but the younger lads and those not familiar with his manner never quite knew how to take him. Poor Steve Smith was out altogether with Nick Youngs claiming the spot on the bench. Nigel Melville had long been a favourite of Budge's; apparently there had been moves to put him in the North team for the game against the All Blacks at Otley in 1979. Melville had understudied 'Smithie' on England's 1981 and 1982 summer tours. However, Melville's long wait was to be extended when an ankle injury cancelled his proposed debut and Steve Smith leap-frogged Nick Youngs straight back into the team. Apparently, our former captain had been left off the bench because his presence might have embarrassed the new scrum-half and new captain – now he was back, but the mood had changed. Heads were down, everyone was looking over their shoulders and even the effervescent 'Smithie' was subdued.

But such a crucial switch of personnel didn't spur our leaders into thinking of changing the game plan. Despite the fact that Scotland fielded a new cap, Tom Smith, and No. 8 Iain Paxton for their second row pairing, England decided to play an expansive game. It shouldn't have taken much to work out that with a better scrummaging unit and the tactical kicking of Steve Smith and John Horton England would need to keep it tight and drawn in Scotland's impressive back row – Jim Calder, David Leslie and John Beattie. Sadly, Steve Smith recognised all too well the return to the suspicious 'seventies and rather timidly curbed his natural style to follow orders. If he had thought that this would buy him international time, he was drastically mistaken. England went down in the Calcutta Cup and 'Smithie' was made to carry the can again after a match in which he had done exactly what the selectors wanted and did not kick the ball once.

If a player of his experience doesn't feel confident enough to trust his own judgement and ability, small wonder that the rest of the team followed suit. Suddenly, in half a Championship, England had stepped back a decade and the blame must lie fairly and squarely on Budge Rogers and his selection panel, who had shown the players no confidence, no loyalty, no consideration and very little regard. Worse was to follow in Dublin. We didn't do too badly in the first half, but had a disastrous period shortly after and were well beaten in the end. In all, England had managed a solitary try in the Championship: of their 55 points, 42 had come from my penalty points with our fly-halves adding three dropped goals. The journey from Championship favourites to flops had been dramatic, torturous and unexpected.

The Dublin result meant that Ireland shared the Championship with France, despite having been heavily defeated in Cardiff. Scotland had been saved a whitewash at our expense and Wales' position in the middle of the table would have been at the top had they won in Paris. As for England, we were out on our own with that lonely drawn point against Wales our only reward. All the hard work of the previous three years had gone to waste and although it was difficult to see it at the time, Mike Davis was as much a victim as we were, suffering from the same erosion of confidence that had been inflicted on us by the rest of the selection committee. We hadn't played our part on the field, but Budge Rogers had a lot to answer for.

Budge had been a permanent fixture in the English side in the 'sixties and was respected for all he had achieved on the rugby field. But he had such a naive idea of what was needed to compete at the highest level that his prowess as a selector was always in doubt and he tended to let personal differences interfere with his judgement on a player. Any lingering doubts about Budge Rogers disappeared on the tour of the States when he was manager: all his shortcomings were exposed and by the time we returned home the England players were wondering how the fortunes of English rugby could be in his charge. He had absolutely no sympathy with or for the players and I'd been treated more like an adult on school outings. We seldom travelled with him in America because he had been provided with a free Jaguar, though we were usually glad to be rid of him. In almost every matter, Budge would be against us, frightened that we might think ourselves too important. Our daily allowance took care of our food and a weekly call home; there was none of the special treatment traditionally found on a tour of South Africa or New Zealand.

We had many problems with the humidity in the States, not least because our training kit very quickly defeated the most powerful air fresheners. It really needed a journey to the laundry every day and,

113

while the Americans could not afford the extra expense, Budge had an allowance from the RFU to cover additional emergencies like this. Nevertheless, we ended up doing deals with maids so that our rooms didn't become health hazards. Training in sweaty, smelly kit is never pleasant, so we paid the laundry bills ourselves. Budge then turned to Peter Wheeler, Clive Woodward, Les Cusworth and me: 'The trouble with you Leicester boys is you can't tour!' he said. No wonder Budge would never have Peter Wheeler as captain. So while the playing side may have looked good, the atmosphere in the squad was so tense that it was going to take very little to upset the fragile harmony. And this was before 'boot-money', the Slemen scandal and the sacking of Steve Smith!

'Smithie' attempted to explain the mood of the players after the Scotland defeat and their sense of betrayal, especially by a chairman of selectors who could slag off his own players immediately after a match when he had made sure the captain was not going to be there to defend himself and his team. When Steve did try to defend himself he was accused of being irresponsible and of having helped to destroy team spirit. As far as we were concerned, the selectors had needed no help on that score.

For the Irish match David Trick had been brought in to replace Tony Swift in Mike Slemen's spot – or so we thought. But even in Dublin, neither winger knew which side he was playing on. J.C. was the senior man and, with the Lions' selection due a couple of days after this, he saw little point in switching over after 19 internationals on the right flank just because the selectors had created their own mess on the left. Quite rightly, he stood his ground and newcomer Trick was the one to play out of position. Before this downward turn, the England pack had looked like providing the Lions with the bulk of their forwards, but our relatively lightweight scrum had found it tough going all season. The Lions' tour kept the lads battling away, but as England suffered, so did the players' chances of making the trip. Steve Smith was eventually to captain the British Lions in a provincial match, but what a season he had had in the white jersey – captain, then out altogether, next brought back to fill another man's shoes before, finally, England's most-capped scrum-half found himself on the bench for the Irish match with Nick Youngs taking his place.

114

In the end, all Scotland and Ireland had to do to beat us was organise themselves reasonably well. France had chosen their best team, and Wales were still trying to find their feet and were being kept in the hunt by the presence of Jeff Squire and Terry Holmes. But with such a competitive club scene that only meant that coach John Bevan was getting his combinations together. Mike Davis said he turned the 'wine into water' in his four-year reign as England coach, but really the process took less than 12 months. The problems started in North America where the players saw that Budge Rogers couldn't handle pressure or the players – and that tour was a picnic compared to the usual hurly-burly of international rugby. After the Grand Slam, it seemed as if we had made some progress in terms of getting together and working together, but now we were back at opposite ends of the room again. We had lost confidence in English rugby's three most important people – the president, the chairman of selectors and the coach. By the following season the entire trio had retired to the back benches of English rugby and the national team was again 'under new management'.

8

LIONS TAMED BY KIWIS

Nobody needed to tell me that 1983 marked my final chance of making a Lions' tour. Unlike three years earlier, I was confident of receiving the selectors' favour this time. My three challengers – Mark Wyatt, Peter Dods and Hugo MacNeill – were all relatively inexperienced and none could match my record as a goal-kicker. Yet, with the prolific Ollie Campbell around at fly-half, there was always the likely danger that goal-kicking might not be regarded as a priority when choosing the two full-backs. It didn't help that England had been going through a rough patch, especially when our sole reward in the 1983 Championship was a draw at Cardiff, and this after being hailed as favourites for the title. Fortunately, I managed to keep my form and set a new England record of 42 points in the Five Nations Championship.

The Lions' management had been chosen the year before; Willie John McBride, who had been put forward as coach and manager, was given the latter post. Jim Telfer was given the vote as coach ahead of Mike Davis. Telfer had done a sound job with Scotland and had the loyal support of his players. McBride was a rugby legend with five Lions' tours behind him, the last as skipper of the all-conquering 1974 team in South Africa. Both had toured New Zealand and were young enough not to be victims of the traditional generation gap that plagues communications and relations between players and officials. We felt a bit sorry for Mike Davis, whose record until that last season was very impressive; as with some of England's players, everything went wrong for him on the final run-in. His reputation of being too friendly with his players would not have been looked upon as an asset, either.

Those two choices were generally well received; the real controversy and debate raged over who should be the captain. Until his premature retirement on medical advice Bill Beaumont looked

116

certain to become the first man ever to lead two Lions' tours. As with Mervyn Davies' injury in 1976, Billy's withdrawal in 1982 deprived the Lions of their natural leader and meant that the following battle for the ensuing Championship would also include a fight to be skipper. Invariably, the Lions' selectors pick the captain of the leading home country and 1983 was no exception. Their choice was hooker Ciaran Fitzgerald who in 1982 had taken Ireland to their first Triple Crown for 33 years and the year after to a share in the title. Those credentials alone would have made him a firm contender, but the absence of any serious challenger who conformed to traditional guidelines made it a one-horse race. This bare fact did not hinder or prevent wholesale speculation about the choice.

England used two skippers in the Championship – John Scott followed Steve Smith – but neither found any success. Scotland did likewise with prop Jim Aitken succeeding Roy Laidlaw, but Aitken's triumph in the Calcutta Cup came too late – McBride and Telfer had already decided on their man by then. Had Scotland's Grand Slam come a year earlier, Aitken might have been their choice. Wales had a new leader, No. 8 Eddie Butler, but he failed to meet the management's prime requirement – as did all national captains of the 1983 Championship – of being able to command a Test place. McBride had said so in January and it was behind most critics' search beyond Fitzgerald. The two names which came to the fore were Peter Wheeler and Jeff Squire. Jeff was a vastly experienced forward at the peak of his powers, and had led Wales at three different stages of his career. He probably ruled himself out by originally being unavailable before he was persuaded to make a third Lions' trip. The management wanted someone who had been dedicated to the cause right from the start. That left 'Brace'; Leicester and Midlands knew he was the man for the job – top players from all four countries agreed, even the Irish. But our hooker had never been able to convince the England selectors and without their support the Lions were never going to take the risk. Sadly, the Lions felt his presence might be an embarrassment and he was left at home altogether. The All Blacks had to wait until the autumn to see Peter Wheeler's leadership qualities!

So Fitzgerald was given the job. After his success uniting the Irish effort, his performance in New Zealand was very disappointing.

117

He totally misunderstood the duties of a major tour captain; half the time we never saw him as he kept himself to himself, out of the way in his room, and it wasn't until the last day of the tour that he got involved with the other Irish lads in a sing-song. We wondered why he hadn't started that way; you've got to be one of the lads from time to time, if only to be aware of the mood of the party as a whole. Maybe his full-time role as captain in the Irish army had conditioned him to existing and making decisions on his own. Not many of us outside Ireland knew much about him; he seemed a loner. Yet, after arriving late on the international rugby scene, the new Irish captain had transformed a bunch of losers into Championship contenders. But that was as far as he went; those qualities that might have gelled a Lions' party were never displayed. A Lions' captain has to be many things to many people; a father confessor, a spokesman and a link between the squad and the management. There was a lot he could have done off the field to alleviate the tension and make himself more accepted. Throughout the whole Lions' tour, we had a grand total of three days off. That's ridiculous; we are amateurs and not used to training every day. There must be time away from the training ground so that players can mentally prepare themselves. We were going out like stuffed cabbages and doing what the sergeant-major wanted us to do.

Billy Beaumont had insisted that there were no Sunday training sessions on the tour in South Africa three years earlier, but instead, and just as important, was the 'Sunday School', where the lads relaxed over a drink and a few songs. Those were missing and missed in New Zealand. And unlike Ciaran, Billy had hated being on his own. As captain he wasn't required to share and was provided with a single room – this he thought was the worst part of being skipper. For big matches this was essential, but when he wasn't playing Bill would share and let another Lion have the rare privilege of some peace and quiet, which was especially appreciated by several players – some of the bigger forwards are notorious snorers. Even when in a single room, Bill would always pop into the other lads' rooms to see how they were doing. Bill, in many ways, was not a natural skipper, but had learned a lot, especially in the Grand Slam year. Fran Cotton, Tony Neary and Roger Uttley were alongside him and had all been former England captains, and Bill knew

118

how to tap their vast experience. He and Mike knew when to talk at a session and when to work; that's the way a captain and coach should function – in harmony. The two most successful Lions' teams had that combination working together: Carwyn James and John Dawes in 1971 and Willie John McBride and Syd Millar three years later. On both occasions, too, the manager knew his place and didn't interfere with the running and organising of the playing side.

McBride seemed determined to play a fuller part than that when he was manager and, in retrospect, I wonder whether it was wise to give him the manager's job when he would have preferred to coach the party. Certainly, our captain seemed closer to the manager than the coach: Ciaran and Jim Telfer never appeared to make much of a partnership in preparing the Lions for duty. Ciaran was more in tune with McBride and we ended up with what became known as the 'Irish connection'. Even there, Ciaran took a back seat. Although a loner, the captain didn't appear much of his own man and never stamped his identity on the tour. When a position was in doubt, it was the Irishmen who were given a chance nearly every time – or so it seemed to the English, Scots and Welsh – and that bias could mean the difference between making the Test team or not. The Irish were rather on the defensive, especially towards the English, maybe because most of us had stated a preference for Peter Wheeler as captain during the course of the previous winter. Yet even the Irish lads weren't as close as one might have expected to their regular captain. There was no need to hide that fact that 'Brace' would have been my choice as leader. I thought that even without the England job he was odds-on favourite for this one; not only was he the best hooker on all-round ability – contrary to the views of the Lions' selectors who felt he had 'gone' – but he was an excellent administrator and organiser. Add to that his invaluable experience of two Lions' tours (and seven Tests) and you had a world-class player, respected everywhere – and feared in most places. He wouldn't have needed to have earned the respect of his party or to prove himself as Ciaran had to try to do. Even now – or rather especially now – nearly all the party would agree that he should have been there as hooker and captain.

All this controversy did not create the ideal atmosphere in which to begin a tough tour, especially when we were going to need all the

119

experience we could muster because it was largely an untried squad. Only Graham Price, Jeff Squire, Maurice Colclough and John O'Driscoll had previous Lions' Test experience amongst the forwards. It's hard to explain just how important senior men are on a venture like this. Being a full-time rugby player for nearly three months takes a lot of getting used to – that environment is totally alien to the amateur rugby players' normal surroundings and timetable. The higher you go, rugby for entertainment's sake takes more of a back seat and the more you put into the game; even in the top club scene that commitment is only two nights' training a week and a Saturday afternoon. Suddenly, there you are training with a lot of unfamiliar guys every day – it's a completely strange way of life. The Lions' trip was different even to being away with England. The English lads are always good tourists: I couldn't believe or understand some of the Lions as all they thought about was fitness training. It has to be taken seriously, but you can still have a bit of a laugh while doing it. If some players had showed half what they produced on the training field in the matches, we would have done a lot better.

As ever, the Lions' party was a matter of great speculation and I doubt if anyone could have named all 30 tourists correctly. Telfer went out there with the idea of playing an inside centre in the New Zealand style. I couldn't understand why, because the players weren't there. Then the coach confused everyone by playing both inside centres in the first Test, asking David Irwin to change roles. I couldn't work out the back thinking. The main problem was that although Jim Telfer knew his back play, he didn't read situations as well as you would expect. What made his insistence on playing a second five-eighth so strange was that his selectors had kept at home the man who would have filled the spot perfectly – Paul Dodge. For a second Lions' tour the best-balanced centre in the home countries was left behind; unfortunately for us in 1983, injury did not rule out any of the midfield players and 'Dodgy' wasn't called upon as in 1980. Paul could have fulfilled the role of second fly-half because he'd shown the necessary control for Leicester and England. Another unlucky man was Scotland's Keith Robertson, who'd appeared to be one of the most talented backs in the Championship.

The half-backs and props picked themselves, but there was a

real surprise with the inclusion of lock Steve Boyle. 'Fog', as he became known during the tour, had only come into the England team when Maurice Colclough was injured, and although he cleaned up a little bit around the line-out, Boyle hardly made a shuddering impact on the international scene. Maurice joined him in the second row following a nerve-racking battle to get fit after being carried off with a knee injury in the opening Championship game against France. In the back row the exclusion of David Leslie was a shock, especially as John Beattie, after an unhappy tour in 1980, was given another chance to prove himself. John is a nice chap, but he hasn't torn up any trees in Scottish rugby and, although he started well in Wanganui, he again faded from the scene. The selectors picked two good opensides in Jim Calder and Peter Winterbottom, although Jim played left and right with Leslie for Scotland. The blindside places went to Jeff Squire and John O'Driscoll. J.O'D was no longer quite the outstanding player he had been on Bill Beaumont's Lions' tour. With Iain Paxton joining Beattie at No. 8, England's John Scott had missed out yet again. 'Scottie' was the unluckiest victim of England's poor season which seemed to have affected our forwards most.

I'd been fairly confident of making the tour, despite our poor results; my form was good and I was kicking well. I was one of the few not to be taken to task by the media after our defeat in Dublin, two days before the announcement of the party. That same afternoon Mark Wyatt broke his collar-bone in Paris which put him out of contention. Peter Dods was new in the Scotland team and was still waiting to emerge from Andy Irvine's shadow, so the two full-backs looked to be myself and Hugo MacNeill, who saved Ireland at Murrayfield in front of the selectors early in the Championship. Yet, you can never be certain, and I'd got to a stage in my career where I wasn't too bothered. England had prepared me fully for anything the Lions' selectors could do to me – well, nearly anything. My joy of being picked was tempered by the injustices done to 'Brace' and 'Dodgy'. In a party short of class and experience those two omissions were criminal. The selectors decided that 'Brace' would be best left out altogether, although their second choice, Colin Deans, was an outstanding player. Wheeler would have accepted the understudy role and certainly wouldn't have ruled out the prospect of keeping the skipper out of the Test team. As it was, Ciaran was under pressure to drop himself for Deans long before the end of the tour. Nobody accepts second-best on a British Lions' trip, but it's only at hooker or scrum-half that the captain's position can really prevent the better player from breaking through. The captain should always be a recognised player, not least because if the side loses, the captain, even if he does have a bad game, isn't dropped – as a class player you know he will perform the next time.

My rest before the trip meant missing Leicester's fifth John Player final in six years. As the Lions were meeting in London two days after that clash with Bristol, I don't think the management would have been too pleased if I'd hobbled in to start the tour with even a minor injury. For me the trip was the chance of a lifetime. Clive Woodward on the other hand decided to play in the final; not only had he been with the Lions before, but he needed to prove his fitness to himself and others after a mediocre season. The Leicester players understood my decision – as did most of the committee, though not all. Those I talked to appreciated my position and never put me under any pressure, admitting they would probably have done the same themselves. I hope I didn't take it as far as Steve Boyle, who wrapped himself in cotton wool from the moment the party was announced, so that by the time he emerged eight weeks later he was in no condition to cope with Andy Haden and Gary Whetton in the second game. His sluggish start relegated him to the role of dirt-tracker almost from the beginning.

After playing in the John Player semi-final at London Scottish, I took a month's rest. The final made agonising watching. The Tigers were in control until they let John Carr in for two silly tries. Even more harrowing was seeing my good friend Tim Barnwell carried off in what was to prove his last-ever game.

As usual, leading up to the Lions' tour there were a couple of days of kitting out and receptions in London, although several of us missed the bus taking the squad to see Neil McFarlane, the Minister of Sport – too many of us got into a small hotel lift, which got stuck between floors. There was no such hiding during the first week in New Zealand at Wanganui, the longest seven days of my life. Jim Telfer's reputation had preceded him, courtesy of the Scottish lads, mainly, and that opening week was as torturous as we'd been led to believe it would be. It's the right way to start a tour, the only drawback on this one being that Telfer did not let up for the entire trip. The worst instance was at Christchurch before the first Test when the session lasted three and a half hours – and I was only dirt-tracking. Some days you can't seem to get the training together; it's just one of those things. Telfer's other fault was that instead of telling us to call it a day or to go and play something else, he persevered when it was obvious that we were never going to get it together if we practised until doomsday.

The management never really decided what to do with people like Bob Ackerman. Although they had picked him, he didn't seem to fit into their plans. Bob was a very capable player and turned up powerfully on the wing at the end of the tour. Because he's such a great big lad, people think he's slower than he is, but he showed what the Lions had missed out on against Ireland in 1984, when he scored a try that was positively breathtaking, even allowing for Hugo MacNeill's less than dedicated tackle. But nobody was able to come back and tackle Ackerman and that's quite unusual in international rugby because generally somebody gets back to cover. Roy Laidlaw made a remarkable contribution, especially after the injury to Terry Holmes, but by the finish, the Scottish terrier looked almost punch-drunk. I found him an excellent skipper when he took charge against West Coast at Greymouth. Obviously, losing Terry Holmes during the first Test was a big blow because he was one of the few world-class players we had.

Amongst the forwards, Scots Iain Milne and Colin Deans were the unluckiest; both deserved a Test place by the end of the series. Maurice Colclough never found the form that had made him such a feared member of the 1980 Lions. He had shown great courage in fighting back from injury to make the trip, but after a good start his play deteriorated. Steve Bainbridge emerged as one of the best forwards of the tour after missing the original selection. Sadly 'Beanbags' reverted to his old self when back in an England jersey. Jim Calder and Peter Winterbottom competed well for the openside, with the extra pace of the 'Strawman' winning the day, although Calder joined him in the pack for the third Test. Jeff Squire started the tour in magnificent form. The Pontypool forward had helped his club to their first Schweppes Cup just before the tour and he

123

inspired the Lions in their opening matches, so the selectors must have been glad he changed his mind about going to New Zealand. With Jeff in this form, it made the decision to take the two Scottish No. 8s all the harder to understand; had John O'Driscoll not been injured against Auckland then Jeff would have filled the No. 8 berth in the first Test.

There was some conflict between Telfer and some of his senior players like Squire, Colclough and Price. Telfer said afterwards that although he was not flexible enough, one of his greatest problems was the intransigence of British forwards, who all had separate styles, depending on which country they played for. Forwards seem to get set in their ways more than backs. Initially, we tried the Australian defence, but it didn't prove successful, so we reverted back to the British way. But we did try. We persevered with the idea of playing an inside centre, but had practically abandoned it when John Rutherford gave up his number 10 shirt and moved there. After a brilliant display, injury kept him out of the final international. As far as I'm concerned 'Ruds' should have been fly-half in the senior side, with Ollie Campbell taking over the centre spot. As his Scottish partner was also at scrum-half, it would have made much more sense; it might have been different if Terry Holmes had still been around. At the time we were two Tests down – there was nothing to lose.

My own tour started well. Although Hugo MacNeill was at full-back against Auckland, Wellington and Manawatu, a tally of 49 points had brought me a lot of headlines. Unfortunately for me, Ollie Campbell was hitting the ball with alarming accuracy and the Test team was not going to be short of a kicker with him around. I'd guessed Hugo would get the nod for the first Test – to me that decision appeared to have been taken back home. Injuries had disrupted our build-up, but even allowing for that the forwards were struggling to establish any sort of pattern and the backs were getting ragged and irregular supplies of ball. Our big chance, though, was in that first Test. But the luck of the bounce – as it did for most of the tour – went the All Blacks' way and, despite a tremendous effort by our pack, playing well above themselves, the home team went one up with a 16-12 victory. It was the nearest we came to success and the tour moved steadily downhill, culminating

In New Zealand with the remarkable Ollie Campbell; for some reason the Lions decided to go into the Canterbury match without either of us.

BOB THOMAS

125

in a record defeat in the fourth Test at Eden Park, which completed a horrendous whitewash. After scoring 24 points in the match after the Christchurch defeat, my chance for a Test place came at Southland on the Saturday between the opening internationals. Unfortunately, I was thumped in the back early on and had to come off during the first half; if I'd realised what the rest of the tour was to offer me, I would have showered, changed and caught the plane home. Our week's 'holiday' at the Bay of Islands was spent mainly on the golf course. Unfortunately, there was no need for any clubs because Jim Telfer was using the fairways for our training – with the Press around, it was the safest place. MacNeill had not had a happy second Test, which was lost 9-0 in the Wellington wind, so the full-back spot was up for grabs. Gwyn Evans played against North Auckland and I expected my trial against Canterbury four days before the Dunedin international.

In spite of all the upsets of playing for England over the years, I did not expect to be ignored this time. The team announcement was a 'don't call us' message from the management. I was now surplus to requirements – something similar to a butter mountain. Once the shock had subsided, there was the even more alarming prospect of a struggling touring team meeting New Zealand's champion province without a recognised goal-kicker. Gwyn Evans and Ollie Campbell were unwelcome company in the stand as far as the Lions' hopes went. It was no surprise when the inevitable happened and the Lions crashed to their second provincial defeat, the selectors' crime being highlighted right on the whistle when Hugo MacNeill missed a none-too-difficult conversion which would have levelled the scores.

Considering the Lions missed six out of eight attempts in the course of the game, even the Irish didn't share Willie John's view – 'I don't think the absence of a regular goal-kicker was the reason we lost' – that our manager relayed to the Press afterwards. That unnecessary defeat did little for confidence and the weather finished the Lions off in Dunedin despite tries by Roger Baird and John Rutherford. There was still time for me to damage my collar-bone against Hawke's Bay, the only game I was given in the second half of the tour. No wonder they say going on tour with the British Lions is a once-in-a-lifetime experience never to be forgotten – I'm still having nightmares.

126

Kevin Murphy helps me from the field at the Hawke's Bay match at Napier to end my playing involvement in the Lions' tour because of a sprung collar-bone.

BOB THOMAS

Rugby players, unlike cricketers, do not choose their room-mates; they are moved around. During the trip I was billeted with John Carleton, Trevor Ringland, David Irwin, Bob Ackerman, Clive Woodward, Ian Stephens, Iain Milne, John Beattie, Nick Jeavons and at the very end with Nigel Melville. I was paired with Hugo MacNeill in London before we left; everyone was with some-one from his position then – the real competition hadn't begun. It's better that players do swap around because it prevents cliques and separate groups developing; it helps if a senior player can show a younger, inexperienced lad the ropes and the demands of touring life, especially if he is on his first big tour. Anyone who thinks a major trip is just an extended Easter thrash will fall by the wayside very quickly. How to organise your laundry, how much money to spend and how generally to come to terms with a strange and rather foreign way of life: these are problems which have to be sorted out alongside the battle for a Test place, and there can be other inter-ferences which are even more unwelcome because they can damage team spirit. During the previous season the leading players in Britain were under a general cloud of suspicion after the revelations of the Adidas 'boot-money' scandal. Then, while we were in Palmerston North preparing for the Manawatu game, David Lord announced from Sydney that two thirds of the Lions' party had signed for his proposed rugby circus. The news caused much more panic in the Press corps than in the Lions' party, but after a couple of frantic days, the furore died down as quickly as it had appeared.

One of the few relaxing afternoons of the tour came in a game of golf against the Press at the Bay of Islands. I was helped through the nine holes by John Reason of the *Sunday Telegraph*. John's forth-right style had made him unpopular with many players, but I was one of the few who got on well with him. That may have been because he was on friendly terms with Chalkie White. Chalkie appeared for the final matches of the tour. He has always been forthright himself, but this time he was uncharacteristically indis-creet and got himself into the headlines with comments about McBride and Telfer. I think he had reacted badly to Peter Wheeler and Paul Dodge not being chosen and to his other two Leicester charges, Clive Woodward and myself, receiving less than fair treat-ment. By the time Chalkie came out to New Zealand, 'Woodie' and

COLORSPORT

THE EVENING POST, WELLINGTON

Above: *There weren't many wins for the Lions' team, but our golf side saw off the British journalists.* (Back row: *Roger Baird, Hugo MacNeill, Mike Kiernan, Nigel Melville;* Front row: *me, Nick Jeavons, John Rutherford (capt), Clive Woodward, Steve Boyle.*)
Below: *Rubbing noses the Maori way with help from John Rutherford's right boot.*

129

I had long been deposited on the shelf. Chalkie took it personally that some of his protegés were not involved when he clearly thought that with the state of the touring party they should have been; he took the bull by the horns in rather an emotional style. In a way, England had frustrated his career ambitions as much as Peter Wheeler's. Along with Des Seabrook, Chalkie was the most experienced and successful coach in England, but the pair saw first Mike Davis and then Dick Greenwood by-pass the system and take over the top job in England without having proved themselves at senior level.

The next time the Lions go on tour they should take two coaches, one for the backs and one for the forwards. Most national squads have helpers – Terry Cobner works with Wales' John Bevan, and Jim Telfer used his namesake Colin on the way to Scotland's Grand Slam. Unless there is an experienced Lions party, the burden is too much for one man; we were short of former Lions and that put an extra strain on Jim Telfer. Generally most squads have more experience among the forwards, where players reach a peak later in their careers. And many of them go on to coach. There are few back coaches, which is a shame, because it's probably easier to organise the forwards.

But the Tigers Roamed Free

Despite my travels with England and the Lions, the best tour I've ever been on was Leicester's 1981 centenary tour to Australia and Fiji. The atmosphere and company were magnificent and, importantly, the rugby was hard. Our first match was against Queensland and we went down 12-22, which was a creditable performance in view of their record against visitors – they were the only team, outside New Zealand in the second Test, to beat the 1971 British Lions. Then we won quite comfortably against Suburbs in Sydney. The final match there was against the club champions Randwick, coached by Bob Dwyer, who was recently relieved of his national duties in favour of Alan Jones. I thought we were in trouble when their winger flashed past me for a try early on, but we fought back to win 31-19. The action was fast and furious and had even Chalkie White buzzing. During our Queensland stay we spent some time on the Gold Coast beaches with their acres and acres of white sand. After training, we'd rush down there for a game of volleyball in what were, for us, perfect conditions. The locals thought we were absolutely mad because the temperature was only 70 degrees and they were all huddled up in coats and sweaters. The mad Englishmen of Leicester did not let the side down, though.

Leaving Australia, and the hardest part of the tour, behind we moved on for the final two weeks to Fiji where our wives joined us. Our first match there took place in a temperature near the hundreds, and it was very humid, too. Chalkie kept telling us that it wasn't that hot – that it was all in our minds. My memory of that game as I struggled to stay on my feet is of Garry Adey sitting in his shorts in the stand, guzzling down ice-creams and generally relaxing in the shade. I felt terrible afterwards and I was packed off to bed with dehydration. When it came to my turn to make Adey jealous, the wind and rain were frightening as we took on the local police. Our final match was against the President's XV, which consisted of the best Fijians available – the national team were in New Zealand at the time. We won that match, too, to round off a highly satisfactory trip.

Leicester have had some tough matches against touring teams back at Welford Road. We only narrowly went down to the 1981-82 Wallabies. Generally, touring teams have six matches in England – the international, the four regions and one other. In the past that fixture has gone to the universities or the services. It would be better if the current John Player Cup holders were given that game as a bonus for their achievement. You have got to give the tourists, whoever they are, a game against a side which is not composed wholly of representative players. The Tigers came off second-best when we entertained the Romanians. I have never seen a side in which every single one of the 15 players was tailor-made for his position on the field. The forwards were big and powerful, outside them the backs could really run and they had a man who could kick a football further than I've ever seen it kicked before. They took 30 points from us – and there was little we could do about it.

I can't ever see Romania coming into the Five Nations Championship, but they should certainly have a home and away international with two from the table each year. They certainly adopt the rather negative style of Eastern European soccer teams – against us their game was all method and no flair. Maybe if the Romanians, the

Italians and the Spanish got a foothold in rugby, the game would change – and probably for the worse. But they shouldn't be snubbed – it is only a game after all . . . The situation is something of a dilemma. I would like to see some changes, but if too many are made, rugby will cease to be the game it is. You have to be very careful that you don't destroy it by moving it in one direction too quickly. Maybe it will end up like cricket with a professional top layer, but all I hope is that when I sit down in 15 years to watch a match, there is still a good game of rugby union on show, whether that rugby is semi-professional or much as it is today. By then the 'time trials' might have taken over – if they do, I will be very glad I played when I did. The selectors see players in September and October; if they are not fit, all the official has to say is that unless they get fit, they will not be considered. If it doesn't mean enough to the player to get into shape, then you are better off without him. It is organisation – not fitness – which has let England down in recent years; sometimes we have gone on to the field in a worse state than a club team. At least with Leicester we have had some idea of what we are trying to do.

9

LOST WEEKENDS

Rugby these days, even at the highest level, is still about weekends, still about a social event as much as anything else. Of course, if you are one of the 31 participants in an international attraction then you have to wait until the main bout is over; but win or lose, the aftermatch is usually enjoyable and sometimes memorable. That doesn't apply only to England players or those at senior clubs. At whatever level, even in the 'B' XV of a junior old boys team, the rugby clubhouse frequently becomes a weekend retreat, nowadays for the whole family. Junior and county cup competitions give all players an idea of pressure rugby, what it's like preparing for a big game. There may be a hundred times more people watching England, but the tension is there just the same.

My travels have taken me all over the world, but in many ways a rugby weekend in Port Elizabeth or Auckland is much the same as one in London or Leicester. Often, earlier games are more vivid in the memory, those, for example, which were followed by dinner at the Hilton, when such functions were new and exciting. The longer you go on, the more discriminating you become. Being in the national side is not enough on its own; you want to win, you need to win otherwise there's little point in bothering. Even when you are part of a winning team, past disappointments frequently stop you from going overboard with excitement.

A Lost Fortnight
25 April-10 May 1981, The Tigers' Treble
This was the season I was dropped by England for the fourth time after scoring 30 points in the opening two games of the Championship. Marcus Rose was brought in and made an immediate impact. There was enough happening at Welford Road to keep me busy, with Leicester going for a third John Player Cup in their centenary

year. The Saturday before the final, 25 April, was a special day for me. When I converted Mick Newton's try early in the second half those two points took me past Sam Doble's world record total of 3,651; sadly Sam had died tragically at 33. I was proud to have passed his total at the Reddings, the home of Sam's Moseley club. There wasn't much time for celebrating because we were lambing at the time, but I was glad to have got the record out of the way before our John Player final clash with Gosforth.

The Geordie club had won the cup in 1976 and 1977 and like us were going for the treble. As, if we won, our victories would be consecutive, Leicester had the added bonus of knowing that the trophy would be ours for keeps. Yet, despite our recent record, we went into the final as underdogs with the 'experts' reckoning that Gosforth's pack would give them the edge. We had no problems coming to terms with the role of outsiders. The *Daily Express* had already named us 'team of the year' but Gosforth were determined to show that this award was premature, especially as most of them had formed the Northumberland side that had won the County Championship. As usual we travelled to London on the morning of the match. In our first final, in 1978 against Gloucester, Leicester had stayed in a London hotel on the Friday night. We lost and the lads thought it had been wrong to change our normal routine. Normal service was resumed against Moseley in the 1979 final and London Irish the following year. Sleeping in our own beds helped ease the cup final tension. Our preparation worked again in 1981. Our forwards put in a tremendous effort to subdue the Gosforth scrum. Prop Robin Cowling was playing his last match for us; Robin had been on the winning side when Gloucester beat Moseley in the first final in 1972, and now he had three successes with us. Garry Adey, too, on his final appearance had an outstanding game and his experience at No. 8 helped steady our forwards.

Getting a good start is essential and, with Steve Kenney darting over for a try, the Tigers were 9-0 up after only a quarter of an hour. Instead of making Gosforth work to get back into the game, we eased off the pressure, so much so that just after the interval Gosforth were only three points adrift at 12-9. They kept up the pressure, but the turning point came when they held the ball in the scrum and tried to drive on. That was supposed to be their strength, but this show of might came unstuck when the Tigers managed to wheel the scrum. Steve Johnston was on the ball in a flash, leaving the Geordies floundering. Les Cusworth and Clive Woodward carried on the attack before Tim Barnwell raced the final yards to score. With our 16-9 advantage, Gosforth needed to score twice and there were only 15 minutes left. The score remained that way until the end of normal time, but in the minutes added on for injury another 12 points were put on the board. Firstly, I won a kick and chase race to touch down over Gosforth's line, then their prop Rob Cunningham managed a consolation try. That 22-15 victory meant the cup was ours – for good, although there was some confusion about this for the next couple of days. Our secretary Jerry Day had suggested that the club would be just as happy with a replica, and that the original John Player Cup could be handed back. 'The original pot should be there for everyone to play for,' said Jerry; 'if we kept it, it would only gather dust in a showcase somewhere.' But the players had other ideas and as skipper, Peter Wheeler let it be known that the 'real' John Player Cup was staying in Leicester.

Leicester don't stay in London to celebrate their cup triumphs. We have a few drinks with our wives, who have come down on the committee coach, and some tea at Twickenham before heading back to the Leicester Post House where we have a dinner-dance and stay the night. On Sunday morning the fragile remains of England's top club side appear on Radio Leicester. Then it's off to see the Mayor and parade the cup in public. In 1981 the celebrations did not finish there because the following Friday our Centenary Dinner took place, with a brave squad travelling to Twickenham the day after to take part in the Middlesex Sevens. That was not for me because the England squad was departing for Argentina the same day.

Marcus Rose was unavailable because of exams at Cambridge; the other full-back in the party was Gosforth's full-back, Brian Patrick, my opposite number in the cup final. The centenary dinner was especially memorable, not only because the lads gave me two decanters for breaking the world points record; I can't think too many other clubs have celebrated such an occasion in such style. In fact my intentions for a reasonably early night, so that I could spend some time with Lesley before disappearing on the three-week tour, went rather astray. It was that sort of fortnight – I was just glad to be travelling to the Argentine for a 'holiday'.

French Without Tears
The Weekend of 21 February 1982

Although I'd won a Test place against the Pumas, Marcus was reinstated for the domestic season. I even found myself off the replacements' bench with Wasps' youngster Nick Stringer, the new understudy. So, even if anything did happen to Marcus, there seemed to be no way back now. He did lose form and Nick, although capped as a replacement wing, was selected to make his full-back debut in that graveyard of England number 15s, Paris. But Nick never made it after damaging a hamstring the week before, so I had moved from nowhere through the subs' bench to England full-back for my sixth international career. Someone had rung me the Sunday before the match and said 'are you playing?' I said 'no' because I hadn't heard of Stringer's problem. Still, I turned up at Stourbridge the following night more hopeful than usual. Nick was being treated and was running around with Don Rutherford. By the way he was moving I guessed he was going to be all right by Thursday. Even though I had filled in with the senior team that evening, I was surprised when Budge approached me at the end to tell me that I was playing on Saturday. From that moment I decided 'right, this is when I'm going to prove all doubters wrong'. I had one of those heavier French Adidas balls at home and I practised with it for hours.

We spent the Wednesday night at the Heathrow Hotel. Bob Hesford was the 'duty boy' and told us that the party was due to leave at a quarter to nine the next morning. That was 15 minutes out; John Scott and I were still getting changed in our room when Budge Rogers was on the phone wondering why we weren't on the bus with the rest of the lads. I thought: 'Here we go again, another perfect start to the day'. At least Bob admitted his mistake, so we weren't on the carpet for long.

This was my fourth trip to Paris with England, but sadly we were missing Bill Beaumont for the first away trip in a long time. Steve Smith, after having taken over on a one-off basis against Ireland, was now confirmed as skipper. The argument for and against Peter

Wheeler is well documented elsewhere in this book. Our mood was reasonably buoyant, despite the Irish defeat. The French, we were told by Maurice Colclough, had got themselves into a terrible selection tangle regarding their forwards. A relatively simple penalty chance allowed me to get into my stride and when I scored with a longer, more difficult kick straight between the posts soon after, I knew I was 'hot', to borrow an American expression. Then Mike Slemen saw the French relax after we touched down behind our own line. His quick drop out caught the French napping and he and Clive Woodward raced upfield with the defence trailing.

Eventually 'Woodie' got the touchdown and we had got off to a 12-point advantage. You should never lose that sort of a lead in international rugby, but if there is one place you might, it is in the pressure cauldron of the Parc des Princes. The French bounced back with a great try by Pardo, but we were still 12-6 ahead at the interval. I put over a couple more penalties, to which Jean-Pierre Rives' side replied with a huge dropped goal from Lescarboura and two penalties from Sallefranque. Now we were only three points in front. Another penalty and a final try in the corner by John Carleton after a pass from prop Colin Smart (who was to continue in the forefront that evening), guaranteed victory. I converted that try from the touch-line for a personal tally of 19 points; my only miss had been a penalty from the halfway line. All in all a very satisfying day for W.H. Hare.

Budge Rogers came rushing up to me in the changing-room afterwards and said 'you can call me what you like now'. I replied: 'No comment'. I'd made all the points I wanted to make on the park and hoped my case had been proved conclusively. I just thought to myself 'even they can't drop me after this . . .' Our dressing-room was just one big smile, totally unlike the victory there two years earlier on the way to the Grand Slam. There was a greater relief this time after the Irish defeat and after the loss of Bill Beaumont. The team had seemed lost against Ireland, but we had proved now that the departure of one world-class player, however valuable, doesn't stop the rest of the side playing rugby.

The champagne was flowing freely right from the off. Lesley had come over for the game with Peter Wheeler's wife Margaret; we had a drink before dinner and arranged to meet them at the Moulin

Rouge around midnight. Our general condition was not helped when the pre-dinner reception went on for an hour and a half. Having finally moved to our table, we spent another hour hanging around for the food. Maybe the lads did get slightly out of hand at the dinner, but the long delay in serving the meal meant that we had little else to do but drink wine or champagne, although 'Smartie' did take to the 'Brut' variety rather too readily. By the time the waiters arrived all the wine and bread had gone. We sat at tables of ten, which meant that the side was divided into two teams, so the customary 'boat race' drinking challenges took place. The knotted handkerchiefs were on our heads and there was no doubt a lot of noise emanating from our corner of the room, but this was nothing unusual after an international match. Eventually Maurice Colclough challenged Colin Smart to drink his bottle of aftershave, one of the personal gifts left on the table. Maurice had taken the precaution of substituting his with white wine. 'Smartie' let down the front row by not noticing the switch and downed the real stuff. He was carried out shortly afterwards to hospital, where he had his stomach pumped, and another rugby legend began. Eventually, rather the worse for wear, some of us trooped off to the Moulin Rouge. Trying to find our wives in such an enormous place was hopeless – we thought it might be best if they spotted us, so we decided to follow a Mexican rumba on to the stage. The patrons were then treated to my solo performance of *Onward Christian Soldiers* – strangely, I was not offered a regular engagement there. Eventually, back at the hotel, there was time for one last nightcap.

We travelled back the next day without Colin Smart who had been detained overnight in hospital. Coming out of Heathrow, we said: 'Right, where are we going for a lunchtime drink then?'. There were four of us in a car – Peter Wheeler, Paul Dodge, Clive Woodward and me. 'Woodie' was the one who seriously wanted to go; the rest of us were feeling rather fragile. Anyway, after a couple of drinks, Clive was all for moving on; the remaining trio had all got their second wind – or more probably their third or fourth. I went back to Peter's house and waited for Lesley to come back with Margaret. The next morning, listening to Radio 4, I heard details of the England team having been involved in a riot in Paris. I said to Lesley, 'it's just as well you were over there with me, otherwise you wouldn't have believed me when I told you there was no trouble at all!'.

Disaster Day in Dunedin
The Weekend of 3 July 1983

The third Test is decision-time on any British Lions' tour. On this one, the selectors had made their minds up about me a lot earlier, probably before we left London. Four days before the Dunedin Test, the Lions had met the Ranfurly Shield champions Canterbury in Christchurch in the unofficial international. I hadn't played for two and a half weeks after coming off with a bad back against Southland; this was my final chance to press for the full-back spot in the senior team. But the Lions tumbled to defeat with all three main goal-kickers sitting in the stand. That was the end of the road for me. After a moderate winter, the weather was cold and damp in Dunedin, a place very reminscent of Edinburgh. Taking charge of the dirt-trackers, I decided our training workout should be cut short owing to the torrential rain, and we all came inside.

Back in the hotel, the radio was giving details of roads baking at home in Surrey. Not being involved in the Test team, and with the tour nearing its end, the news from across the world made Clive Woodward and I rather homesick. On Friday, I visited a school and talked to the kids about my life and rugby. Being in New Zealand, though, they were probably fairly familiar with rugby-playing farmers – New Zealand has produced one or two of their own over the years. Later the Lions trained on the seafront, which was a desperate place in the wintry conditions. That weekend all the various supporters' trips had arrived from Britain. Our hotel was packed and it was impossible to get a drink or have any privacy outside your room. On the Friday night the dirt-trackers went out with the manager Willie John McBride; the two Irish replacements 'Ginger' McLoughlin and Donal Lenihan also came along. The coach, Jim Telfer, spotted us coming into the hotel just before midnight; we weren't falling all over the place, but most of us would have had trouble walking in a straight line. Jim often stayed up late, but only to indulge in serious conversations about the problems in rugby and British rugby in particular. We got a real roasting as he pointed out that any of the team or the six replacements could drop

139

BOB THOMAS

The only two Tigers who joined the Lions in 1983 – Woodward and Hare – were soon wondering why they had bothered.

out, especially with 'flu in the damp and miserable Dunedin, and we might be needed. Suitably humbled, we sloped off to bed.

Telfer reminded us that we were due out for the dirt-tracking session the following morning. That workout wasn't as bad as we'd feared, but with the frost all around it was just like preparing for a match at Murrayfield. Then, like on all the other international Saturdays in New Zealand, the dirt-trackers sat in the stands and watched the Lions being beaten. Roger Baird did have the satisfaction of scoring the first British try of the series, but the tourists let their chance go in the first half as Ollie Campbell had a bad off-day and never put the New Zealand full-back, Allan Hewson, under pressure. The Lions went back into the lead shortly after the interval with another try, this time from John Rutherford, but the All Blacks used the conditions to keep our forwards pinned down in their own half. Eventually our defence cracked as Stu Wilson equalled Ian Kirkpatrick's 16-try record for New Zealand. That 8-15 defeat meant the series had gone and the final fortnight was really going to drag, especially for those of us with no part to play.

That night the only official dinner of the tour took place. For that single evening we carted around a special dinner-jacket with a small Lions' badge, all a remnant of the days when the four Home Unions used to travel on tour by luxury liner and there were numerous social and embassy functions to attend. The dinner was not without incident – our manager Willie John McBride made a critical speech about the Lions' itinerary which, in an effort to fill the big stadiums during the week, did not have the big provincial games – Auckland, Wellington and Canterbury – at the weekends. Mickey Steele-Bodger, the chairman of the Four Home Unions' Tours Committee and arguably the most powerful man in British rugby, was present and he, having helped work out the fixtures, was to answer McBride's accusations the following day.

As for me, I went back to the Southern Cross Hotel and had a long chat with Gareth Edwards, whose experiences of Dunedin were slightly happier as this was where the 1971 Lions made their winning start. With the series gone, the lads just wanted to get out of Dunedin; unfortunately, our move to Napier was not until the Monday. New Zealand shuts down on Sundays and Dunedin was like a ghost town. Maybe we had become a ghost team, too.

141

10

BUDGING THE SYSTEM

England's rugby players have had as much trouble with officialdom as they have had with opponents during my international career. At every turn the hierarchy frustrate the natural progression of rugby football. This may lead to forced and premeditated developments which could take the game down different paths.

As ever, problems of communication were present at the highest level. For most of my period as an individual player Budge Rogers was the chairman of selectors. Budge was on a different wavelength from the players and saw things that we didn't. His outstanding quality when he was in charge of England was his ability to get the players' backs up, creating situations from real and imaginary problems. Few chairmen let the coach get on with their job and all want to dabble themselves. Often Budge would go up to Steve Smith and John Scott and tell them they were overdoing their holding act at the back of the scrum. Rugby, as far as administration is concerned, seems caught between the cricket and the soccer systems. In cricket the chairman of selectors relates directly to the captain and in the English soccer side the power is wielded by one man, the manager. Rugby has a chairman of selectors and a coach. Although the coach sits in on selection, it's the chairman who gets the side he wants. It is not enough to say that everybody is working towards the same aim; often a coach is working with material that he would not have chosen himself. Even after giving him his side, the other selectors can't leave well alone and frequently England sessions in the past were a free-for-all with all the selectors not only doing their bit, but being seen to do their bit. It's their job to give the coach the team he wants or a team they think will do better and let him get on with his part unhindered. At one time, there seemed to be more selectors on the field than players, but they got the hint eventually. Their presence only serves to confuse the players. And it hinders the coach who can feel inhibited. Mike Davis did a good job and coped well in such circumstances.

The players look to the coach for guidance and they don't want to be diverted in another direction just because it seems that the chairman of the selectors is pulling the strings. The selectors are not helped by the English system. The men in Wales have three big games each week they can watch, in which they know they can see many top players in pressure situations. In New Zealand, the three selectors have their provincial system and in a match like Wellington-Auckland, perhaps 20 of the participants will be serious contenders for an All Black place. Their English counterparts have to see Harlequins and Northampton, probably only a handful of whose players could be considered for England duty and even these will not be seen in a contest which resembles the international arena in any shape or form.

The best stepping-stone to the top is not the county champion-ship, but the regional matches. These games were only in existence because of foreign visits until the discarded regional competition was reintroduced after the disastrous 1983 and 1984 Championships. Yet, with the North's and the Midlands' victories over the All Blacks – and others – the regions have provided England with most of her triumphs in recent years. Players have no trouble indentifying with the regions, especially where a tradition of doing well against touring teams has been established. If a player doesn't feel pride playing for the Midlands or the North, then he won't feel any when wearing the England jersey. The county championship should be a matter of personal choice; the RFU tried to get the top players to conform at the start of the 'eighties, but because so many top men would not do so, the pressure was quickly abandoned. A four-region championship brings the best 60 players together before the start of the Five Nations matches. A lot of England's momentum for the 1980 Grand Slam came after the North-West Counties had toured South Africa the summer before. The regions already have their own identities and each area is large enough to contain players nearly all of whom would at least have international potential.

Three matches in a regional championship hardly chokes up the season and could lead directly to a final trial. If there was a major touring team in the UK, that championship would not be needed, as long as the matches against the visitors were near the internationals. There is a lot of difference between playing well in September and in the middle of the season. For the clubs, two national leagues then divisional tables would provide a route to the top. Even if the big clubs don't like it, there has to be relegation and promotion, otherwise the whole project is useless. Then, even when certain areas disagree with the choices of the top teams, they can draw consolation from the knowledge that those destined for the top will get there if they deserve to. Promotion would also restrict the number of teams in each league because the matches would need to operate on a home and away basis; for example, 10 teams, with 18 matches in a season. That may sound like cluttering up the already busy schedules of top players, but four matches a year could be played mid-week under floodlights. That system would also help those leading men because they would know which matches were important and would not have to turn out each week on a 'hit and miss' basis. At present April, apart from the final of the John Player Cup, is very much a winding-down month – a lot more could happen. Players continue in France until June. Clubs will still want to continue their traditional fixtures, but I'm not saying that it's up to the club whether the top players want to participate. Last season I only played around 19 games for Leicester and my total for all matches was about 30. The regions have proved themselves, despite opposition from the powers that be, time and time again. When the selectors have transferred that trend into the international side, it has usually been successful. Yet Budge Rogers ignored the evidence of the North's victory over the All Blacks in 1979 and England lost to New Zealand 10-9 a week later.

Many of the problems stem from the generation gap; it takes far too long for players to work up to positions of power from which they can institute changes. By the time they have undergone the long wait, they are generally out of step with what the new player wants because the game has moved forward in the meantime. Rugby has developed very quickly in some areas in recent years. Another problem is that many officials were not outstanding players anyway, often not even playing for England, but deciding at an early age on a career in a committee in which the sole qualification for getting to the top would seem to be time, lots of it, in service.

Once they are entrenched there, you try to shift them. One distant day in 30 years' time one of these people will become president; the top job, whatever that means. Generally, these people are not that successful in business, either. Don't believe that they have sacrificed themselves for rugby; it's just that they have found it easier to compete in an area where it is impossible to show any results for their efforts and is therefore difficult to be judged a failure. Many of the committee members are decent sorts who will come up to you and chat sensibly after a match, whether England have won or lost. Others either bask in reflected glory when you have won or have the answers to all England's problems should you lose. Frequently, I have wondered whether they have actually been watching the game I've just taken part in because what happened bears no relation to what they are talking about. The longer you have been around the England team, the more earbashings you get; maybe they feel that younger players should serve their apprenticeship before being fortunate enough to have the benefit of their advice.

Air Commodore Bob Weighill, the current secretary of the RFU, has always been fair in his role as buffer between the players and the committee. Tradition tends to inhibit the committee. Those members from the forces are often so used to doing things by the book that it really would take a revolution to shift them. England have done well in recent years when players have been selected from one area or when one area has been very strong, and often you will find the officials there are forward-looking and have a good relationship with the players. It's ridiculous that players' and officials' energies should be wasted fighting each other when England is failing to do itself justice on the international field. Basically the players just want to get on with the job, but are constantly distracted by petty squabblings.

11

SPOTS OF BOTHER

Sporting life is rarely without incident, but England's rugby men seem to have been seldom out of the limelight in recent times, much of the exposure being due to activities off the field. Often these controversies have diverted our attentions and energies away from the job in hand – there are enough distractions as it is without further aggravation between players and officials. Their attitude towards us ranges from suspicion to gentle, but unswayable paternalism. Many of these problems have been dealt with elsewhere in the book, like the complaints made when I moved from Notts to Leicester, a decision I took to further my representative career. I have also mentioned my reaction to Dickie Jeeps' speech after the North and Midlands' victory over the 1976 Argentinians, the game that finally made up my mind on the question of the move to Leicester. Jeeps' amazing criticism of our winning performance when he said that he would rather have lost than won in the way we did had a familiar ring to it. But, as rebel England prop Mike Burton pointed out when all the officials and former players were condemning the proposed David Lord circus, nobody was asking them. Nobody was asking Jeeps to play – his days on the field were over – winning was our business now and we were entitled to seek it in our own way.

Other more general arguments like club versus county have also been discussed earlier. Although Leicester were considered to be a hotbed of anti-county feeling, I played for Notts, Lincs and Derbys until the new system came in, with matches being played on Saturdays. David Brookes, then the president of the RFU, made a speech at the Leicester Centenary dinner calling on the club to accept the new county championship formula; Peter Wheeler, our captain, stated the club's view fairly accurately, pointing out that Leicester provided more competitive rugby, but there was no real flare-up when many decided to ignore the county scene. One conflicting Saturday is now our club game with Swansea, one of the best matches of the season and a far more competitive game than you were likely to get for the county . . . and far more enjoyable. A disappointment in 1984 was when Leicester went down to Cardiff on the same day that England met Australia. But had the county scene not changed from midweek, I would have carried on. Only when there was a straight choice between club and county did I stick with the Tigers. Also, it's easier to get away with playing two matches a week when you're younger; it's not simply a question of physical fitness which prompts you to pace yourself as time goes by. Originally, the county games were in midweek in the Midlands because the top clubs – Leicester, Coventry, Northampton and Moseley – had all their important matches at the weekend. If the county championship reverts back to the old way, I'm sure many players will take up county rugby again.

Often a fuss is made out of nothing. That was exactly what happened when news leaked out that Derek Morgan, the new chairman of the England selectors, had sent me a letter during the British Lions' tour of New Zealand. The word went out that he was unhappy with the way the England players had been treated on the trip by the selectors and he wanted to know why. In fact, all he said in the letter was that there was a change of style at the top, selection-wise, as far as England were concerned, and that he wished the boys well for the rest of the tour. He made no mention of the Lions' tour and our part in it. It was really a note of encouragement for the following season – nothing more than that. All the fuss was really pathetic. And because of all that and the rumours about dissension in the camp, we showed the letter to the Lions' manager Willie John McBride, to prove that it contained nothing critical or contentious, in order to keep the peace in all quarters.

Very few incidents have spoilt my time with Leicester. Apart from one upset, the trouble has involved the club rather than me personally, as when secretary Jerry Day suggested we might be happy with a replica of the John Player trophy after we had gained permanent possession of it with a third successive victory in 1981. Jerry was out of step with the mood of the rest of the club who, like him, had worked hard to earn the trophy. Leicester had been in the headlines before the final the previous year when we were banned from wearing the jerseys we had used at Twickenham a year earlier. During a Press conference, Bob Weighill caught sight of one of our jerseys, worn by a model, and spotted the logo plus the name Europa. The logo was permissible but the name was not. Again, we were unhappy, but the manufacturers agreed to find us a new set of jerseys.

I was to find myself at the centre of things just before I left for the Lions' tour of New Zealand. After playing in the John Player semi-final win over London Scottish, I called it a day and this gave me a five-week break before the tour. I took the children to watch the home game against Neath and was mucking around with them on the grass after the match. Our skipper Steve Johnston came over to me and asked if I was coming in for a drink in the sponsors' room. I answered that I wasn't that thirsty, and anyway hadn't played. He told me not to be silly, so I went in with the kids. While on my first pint and talking to someone else, the sponsor came up to me, demanding to know if I had played today and did I intend to play again before I went to New Zealand. When I answered 'no' to both questions, he said: 'I don't want you drinking in my bar then'. I told him that I'd been invited in by the skipper. The bar was fairly packed and I didn't want to make a fuss. I just put down my drink and left. I passed Steve Johnston on the way out. I told him what had happened, and the word quickly spread round the rest of the lads. Their response was tremendous and, to a man, they left the bar. The Neath boys followed a few minutes later. The sponsor was left with plenty of space in his bar. I was grateful for the boys' loyalty, but it was such an unnecessary affair, especially when it gained national prominence in the Press. What was more distressing was that it was so untypical of the atmosphere at Leicester, which has remained a homely club despite its recent success. I'm glad to say it has been the only incident of its kind that has soured my time at Welford Road.

Often players are merely pawns in a far bigger battle, as in the South African question. The trouble is that almost everything you can say about the apartheid problem has now become a cliché, but I still don't see why, when business still carries on with South Africa, sportsmen should be discriminated against. It always amazes me how petty people can get. The Leicester Council were very aggrieved that some of us should want to go there and represent our country. While complaining about the lack of rights in South Africa, they wanted to deny us ours by preventing us from going. Obviously, there are many factors to be taken into consideration other than rugby, but it is to be hoped that people will always react against being dictated to, whether here or in South Africa. One off-hand remark made on our return was that the England rugby team were unlikely to be put on any 'blacklist' because, in the course of our horrendous defeats, we had gone out of our way to avoid any sporting contact with South Africans!

Over the years I have learned to be cautious in my dealings with the Press. Often it's not that they actually misquote you, but they will leave out a qualifying statement so that the quote has greater impact. For example: 'Dick Greenwood made lots of mistakes in his first season, but that's only to be expected as part of the learning process'. Take away the second half of the sentence and it looks like you've got it in for the coach. But, in general, most of the players get on with the media men; you soon get to know those who will let you down. As with the players around you, it becomes obvious what their strengths and weaknesses are. However, some officials are foolish enough to allow no contact at all; it's far better to work with the Press rather than against them. The foreign Press is much the same, but you have to be especially careful when travelling abroad as a British Lion or an England rugby international. At these times I found I was really under the microscope; every incident was exaggerated to fill the front page, a spot in which rugby often finds itself in some countries. Sometimes the pressure for a story makes a journalist break a confidence or create something out of nothing. In South Africa in 1984, we were supposed to have half-wrecked the Elizabeth Hotel after our first Test defeat. The following week, back in Britain, the *Sunday Express* claimed that one of the five new caps in that match had warmed up for the most important day of his sporting life by gulping down 21 bottles of beer. Stories as ridiculous as this are hardly worth bothering about, but they can still tarnish the team's reputation – some people will always insist there's no smoke without fire. A similar situation arose in New Zealand when news of a fight between John Beattie and Jeff Squire on the team bus broke at home. Again, it was mere conjecture, and the journalist concerned was to find himself ostracised for his negligent behaviour. The trouble is that pressures and circumstances change, and a lot of journalists who are former players seem to expect the game to remain as it was in their day. They don't appear to appreciate that the pressures are far greater now and the days when a Lions' tour consisted of a leisurely sea voyage followed by six months of cocktail parties and rugby matches are long gone. Nowadays there are more journalists than players on tour – and every one of them is looking for a story. I often think the media men have a better time than the players do – and they get paid for it!

The Press certainly had a field day when news of the Adidas 'boot-money' scandal broke at the beginning of the 1982-83 season. The whole affair was a prime example of the authorities' failure to deal with a situation that should never have arisen. All the major boot companies had tried to make deals with the RFU, but Twickenham maintained that boots were a personal item of clothing and had to be the choice of the individual. As soon as allegations of payments were made, this 'right' went straight out of the window. All the players were suspected of having their hands in the till and had to pay penance by having all markings blacked out before internationals. In the meantime, the authorities desperately sought to make the deal with the companies that they had been rejecting for years. But, because they were as suspicious of all the established manufacturers as they were of the players, in the end the RFU signed an agreement with Nike, a firm that was not even producing rugby boots at that time. Having got themselves into this situation, the Union then made the players feel like criminals. Had it not been for one or two sensible officials certain players would have been used as scapegoats without the slightest evidence of their guilt.

Many members of the older brigade see guarding rugby union's archaic amateur laws as a relentless campaign against modern players, who are, they seem to think, bent on destroying the game that has brought them success. That's exactly how they viewed David Lord's proposed 'rugby circus' in 1983; again they overreacted, threatening immediate expulsion to anyone seen in the same town as Lord. New Zealand eventually had other ideas and Andy Haden's communications with the entrepreneur were given the Board's blessing at Haden's 'trial' late in 1984. Had the Union done their sums, they would have realised that they had little to fear from Lord. As he was offering around £91,000 a man, he would have needed something like £20 million to get the event off the ground. As the biggest sponsorship in British sport is Canon's involvement in soccer, which represents one million pounds over three years, Lord hadn't a prayer of getting his professional rugby circus off the ground. Had he done so – with that sort of money involved – every international rugby player in the world would have been interested.

One of Lord's assertions was that he would also have brought together international rugby's top referees. The world's leading players would not have argued with that, although it's safe to say that hidden away at the back as I am, I have very little to do with the men with the whistle. That doesn't stop me getting frustrated with them, especially the officious types who stop Leicester's free-flowing style. The biggest change in my time has been that most referees now seem to be continually watched and assessed, which means that most of them spend the match refereeing for somebody in the stand, not the players on the field. I would much prefer the system used abroad where both teams send in reports on the referee – after all they are the people most affected by his performance. The referee is there only to help 30 players have a game of rugby. I have always preferred the French referees like Monsieur Bonnet, who took charge of our Grand Slam match at Murrayfield. Afterwards, it seemed that he had blown his whistle only four times – to start and finish each half. Norman Sanson, who refereed his last match at Leicester, was one of the best and his decision to give up was a great loss to the game. There are not so many good referees around that you can afford to lose someone like him. When I first went to Wales with Notts and Leicester, the officials were very much 'homers', but in recent years there has been a great improvement. Fundamentally, I see the referee's role as using his discretion to control the game 30 players are trying to put together.

Referees also have to cope with outside pressures, like knowing that if they send off an Englishman they will have ended his international aspirations for the season. That seems an unfair burden – and punishment. In Scotland, a frequent offender will receive such

England players were accused of being in the middle of the Adidas boots row – there seemed to be no escaping those controversial three stripes.

a long ban that he will be virtually ruled out anyway. Why should someone given his marching order in September face what amounts to a nine-month ban, while the same offence committed at the beginning of April might carry only a four-week penalty? At Leicester you can always tell if the referee is nervous. Firstly, he comes into the dressing-room by two o'clock, when half the team hasn't yet turned up, already changed and wanting to speak to the skipper and check the studs. The more experienced man will pop in about half an hour later, calling 'studs, lads', and with the minimum of fuss will simply pass his hand along the bottom of the boots. Generally, referees should be allowed to use their discretion as regards how the game is played and should not feel under examination all the time. It's the spirit of the law, rather than the letter, which gives spectators the sort of match they come to watch. Another problem is the varying standard of the matches they are expected to take charge of. The system whereby everybody does their share of the less senior games is wrong; the top players want the top referees – there, at least, David Lord had it right. Like players, referees need competition to keep their edge. What with referees, Press, officials and administrators, it's a relief to get on the pitch and only have the opposing team to worry about!

12

THE BEST OF THE REST

I may have ended up as England's most-capped full-back, but for a lot of the time after my 1974 debut I was second or third choice, if I was lucky enough to be in favour at all. In the early days my rivals were Tony Jorden and Peter Rossborough; towards the latter half of the 'seventies, Alastair Hignell became the flavour of the month. Peter Butler and David Caplan appeared when Hignell was troubled by injury. And, after I played a part in the Grand Slam, Marcus Rose materialised as the boy wonder – when he faded from the scene, Nick Stringer became my understudy for my last two seasons.

Peter Rossborough was a natural footballer, very talented, though not as reliable as Tony Jorden. He was very much the old-style defender at the back. It was Peter who added that extra something to the attack which Tony lacked as England searched for counter-attacking full-backs. Neither ever really established himself as a regular successor to Bob Hiller. Peter Butler was a marvellous goal-kicker, though a little suspect in defence. But with a good enough side you can go into a game with a match-winning kicker without needing anything else from the number 15 shirt. Orrell's Dave Gullick was a typical gritty full-back – I remember playing with him in the centre in an England schoolboy trial – and he was a bit unlucky not to be capped. Alastair Hignell was the first to find a regular spot at full-back. Alastair was also solid in defence, a good tackler with good hands, but he couldn't punt the ball very far. I always felt that lack of distance put his side under unnecessary pressure. He was always safe, but struggled to take his team out of their own half; importantly, he was no more than an able goal-kicker. Alastair had a good personality, but in picking him the selectors showed just what they thought of me at the time because he was actually a converted scrum-half. It all depends on what they want from their full-back; sometimes all they require is someone secure, safe and sure. Other times, they feel the threequarter line needs a boost, an extra attacker; often they choose someone adequate in all those departments who can kick goals. David Caplan's brief run was ended by injury, although he has returned in the last couple of seasons to play for Northampton. He was a full-back who liked to counter-attack and had obviously been helped by the presence of John Spencer and Ian McGeechan at Headingley when he played there.

My personal duel with Hignell – coincidentally, we had both played county cricket – came to a head during the England tour of the Far East in 1979, and I took a mandatory eight count. I played in the first Test against Japan, but was left out after that. With the new regime of Rogers and Davis in attendance, my future did not look all that bright. Yet Alastair never played for England again as his injury problems increased. My next adversary was a young Cambridge student who had Leicester connections, Marcus Rose. He'd been an outstanding schoolboy international and was an excellent ball player. But, after making the highest grade, his Cambridge rugby did not give him enough discipline to do his job properly, although few have made such an impact as he did on his debut in Dublin. But a year later – also against Ireland – his carefree attitude helped give away two tries. Still, the ability is there and if he knuckles down the promise of his early games for England could finally be realised.

Nick Stringer has come a long way fast. He remains erratic, probably due to his inexperience. One minute it looks as if he can't miss with goal-kicks, the next it seems as if he's aiming at the corner flag. Nick is big, quick and can look a world-beater. Yet he doesn't always inspire confidence. It's difficult to put your finger on it; he just lacks the consistency you expect from an international full-back. In one game, he can look the answer to all the problems; in the next he creates most of his own. The opponent I most admired at full-back was Andy Irvine. J.P.R. Williams was a legendary character, so solid, but I always worried and wondered what Wales would have done without goal-kickers like Barry John and Phil Bennett at fly-half. A full-back's job is primarily defence, and J.P.R. could not be faulted there; his tackling was frightening and he never looked like dropping a high ball. If I was making a composite of the best full-back in the world, then it would consist of J.P.R.'s defence, Andy Irvine's attacking ability and, if I may be permitted, my goal-kicking. Others who have impressed me include Frenchmen Jean-Michel Aguirre and Serge Blanco.

This book allows me the unique privilege of being an England selector all on my own – I'm able to choose from a 25-cap career, as well as guaranteeing myself the full-back spot, which hasn't always been the case. My choice for the right wing has to be John Carleton, with Peter Squires very unlucky to miss out because the pair are two of the best England backs of recent times. J.C. has been a particular friend, on and off the field, and we've worked well together in defence. John is very strong in attack and, although Peter Squires was probably better at beating men in close situations, J.C.'s all-round play is more effective. That try he scored in loose play from the scrum-half spot against Wales in 1982 showed his ability and opportunism. Although David Trick and Tony Swift are basically right wingers, they have been required to play on the left, but I wouldn't put them in the same class as J.C. On the other flank, most of my games have been with Mike Slemen and, as with J.C. we have formed a good defensive unit. My first cap was played with David Duckham; I admired him greatly and remember him doing a lot of damage for Coventry against me in a club game once. Like Mike, David was a world-class player, but as most of my successful days were spent with the former, 'Slem' gets the nod. It was a disgrace when he was left out in 1983, especially considering his two previous games for England. In Paris the season before, his fast drop-out had led to Clive Woodward's try, then Mike's quick throw-in resulted in John Scott being tackled without the ball and I was able to kick the penalty. That's not a bad contribution for a winger and against Wales he scored in the corner to set us on our way. It wouldn't have been so bad if there had been someone to replace him, but the selectors spent the season trying to make do with Swift and Trick. It was all so unnecessary. The two challengers to his position in 1984 were at least left wingers – Rory Underwood and Mark Bailey – and that pair will be doing battle for some years to come.

There is no need to go any further than my Leicester colleagues Paul Dodge and Clive Woodward for a centre pairing. Equally talented players have filled England's midfield in my time, but nobody can match their partnership. Paul has always been the solid, dependable type, the perfect foil for Clive's rare and sometimes wayward wizardry. Clive probably needed Paul more because there are few with his poise – the former could go off on his wanderings, knowing that Paul Dodge would make sure any gaps were plugged. Clive Woodward has the ability to confuse and tear apart the toughest international defence, but such talents are based on confidence and without it, he has occasionally been reduced to the ranks of the ordinary. But you must have faith in someone who can lift a game to the heights very few can reach. Tony Bond was a powerful centre and it all might have been very different for him had he not broken his leg at the start of our Grand Slam season. Although Huw Davies has turned up in England's midfield, I regard him as basically a fly-half. The pairing on my debut was Geoff Evans and Keith Smith; both were troubled by injury and Smith's promising career was ended before it really began – England were the poorer for that. Andy Maxwell suffered the same fate as Smith in my second international against France when a knee injury finished his career completely. His co-centre, Barrie Corless, may have lacked flair, but worked hard on his strengths, an example of how dedication and commitment can promote a player to fill a role for his country at the highest level.

Nick Preston was an elusive runner, but his hands were poor. Bryan Barley looked the part when he came in during the 1984 Championship, but after injury he tried too hard to make an immediate impression in South Africa and struggled. John Palmer took his chance after being so near for several seasons. John is a great asset to any club. He is versatile and dependable, but he lacks that extra bit needed to establish him at the very highest level. Alan Old is out on his own as my fly-half; he possessed all that was required of a first-rate pivot. Alan could read a game so well and had the ability and rugby brain to take control. Few men had a better sense of humour and even fewer had his will to win. He made an enormous contribution to our Grand Slam, although for him it was spent on the replacements' bench. And despite the fact that John Horton did an excellent job that year, I always felt Alan Old was the man who should have had that role. The other quality about Alan which set

BOB THOMAS

I may be Hare by name, but I've been running short of the stuff in recent years and Ireland's Phil Orr should know better than to try to grab me there.

him apart from other England fly-halves was confidence. John Horton and Les Cusworth have been good number 10s, but neither has been able to establish that ability to read a game and take it by the scruff of the neck. England are still looking for a fly-half with the confidence to do that. Les is a talented player, but has just missed out on being a great fly-half. Had he kicked better tactically and read the game quicker, Les would have been England's fly-half for years. Huw Davies made a tremendous impact on his first season and was outstanding in Argentina, keeping John Horton out of the side. Sadly he has made very little progress since then. Huw is a good footballer and a very strong tackler, but he seems to have great difficulty in keeping up his concentration for 80 minutes. In the beginning, he was going to be England's fly-half for a decade as well as a future captain, now he has let others less gifted than himself assume his position.

Steve Smith is my scrum-half choice of the five I have played with. Jan Webster appeared with me only in my debut match, but his record was impressive, especially those victories in South Africa and New Zealand at the start of the 'seventies. Malcolm Young was the first England scrum-half to play ten consecutive games for a long time; I got back into the side near the end of his career. Malcolm worked well with his Gosforth team-mates Roger Uttley and Peter Dixon, but had Steve Smith got himself in gear this talented half-back could have played over 50 times for England. After a promising start in 1973, Steve became *l'enfant terrible* for a while, wasting his many talents by not keeping in shape. He had everything, a strong pass, a good physique, the ability to read a game; he was full of confidence and had a powerful left foot. His only fault was that he eventually overplayed his hand in working with the back row in general and John Scott in particular. But that shouldn't detract from a memorable career. And off the field, Steve Smith was the best comedian I've ever come across. Nick Youngs and Richard Hill – and not Nigel Melville – were his successors while I was around. Nick is another strong lad, with bags of confidence, but he needs to improve his pass. That is not a vital hindrance – Gareth Edwards had to overcome similar problems. Richard Hill has come a long way fast, but is very dedicated, and if he continues to progress he should be to the fore for some years to come.

Front row play has always been something of a closed book to me, but I can't choose a better unit than our Grand Slam trio – Fran Cotton, Peter Wheeler and Phil Blakeway. I will stay with 1980 for my second row – Bill Beaumont and Maurice Colclough. Although he played with me only in my debut game, Chris Ralston was a line-out forward who was something special. Nigel Horton was another top-class competitor – he could very easily have taken Maurice's place for the whole Grand Slam, not just the opening match. Maurice was a tower of strength, but struggled with injuries in his final season and was distracted more by his mental efforts than by his role in the engine-room of the scrum. References to Bill Beaumont are numerous in this book – it is sufficient to say here that his premature retirement troubled England more than anything else in the 'eighties. Steve Bainbridge has an athlete's build and was voted the most improved forward after the Lions' tour in 1983 – unfortunately, there was little sign of that improvement the following season for England when he was a big disappointment. His physique is very similar to that of New Zealand's Gary Whetton – sadly the resemblance ends there. John Fidler served England well on his tours to Argentina in 1981 and to South Africa three years later. 'Fids' did his job with the minimum of fuss and showed a lot more pride in playing for his country than some of the up-and-coming prospects. Steve Boyle was a lucky man – three England caps and a Lions' tour. That is not to say he didn't have ability, but he seldom used it for as long as 80 minutes. He has a lot of talent, but is basically lazy. Jim Syddall was unlucky that year, having been counted out after a sending-off. 'Evil Eric' could be over-boisterous at times, but he was a difficult man to compete against.

John Scott, despite his *menage à trois* with the ball and 'Smithie' in 1983, is my No. 8. Andy Ripley and Chris Butcher are similar individual types. I am not ignoring Roger Uttley because he is the perfect man for the blindside spot. That is where he served the Lions on their unbeaten trek to South Africa in 1974 and England in their Grand Slam year. Roger had a great knack of being able to tidy up any loose possession so that it was not bobbing around causing chaos; he seemed to have time while others were being hurried. It's sad to leave out Peter Dixon, the only person to have played in all of my first three international matches – in some ways his international career was as disjointed as mine. Eventually, he learned from Twickenham's mistakes, retiring on the night of the North's victory at Otley, knowing that the next day the selectors would get it wrong again. Nick Jeavons filled Roger's shoes to some extent and of the three blindsides who played in the 1984 Championship, John Hall was by far the best.

Mike Rafter has never once failed to live up to his name of Rafter the Grafter, but his main trouble was that he lacked the size needed for international rugby; still he remains one of the great characters of the England scene and I have always enjoyed his company. But my openside flanker must be Tony Neary, which means I have picked the Grand Slam pack *en masse*. Neary was a magnificent forward and I would even put him ahead of Fergus Slattery, Graham Mourie and Jean-Pierre Rives – I can't pay him a higher tribute than that. David Cooke is another good club footballer who just lacked that little extra needed to make the final step to the top. Still, David is a much better player now than he was when first capped for England in 1981. Peter Winterbottom is a very destructive influence on his opponents and has a different style to Tony Neary's – I don't know many flankers who get as physically involved as Peter. But I think he is going to find himself under a lot of pressure from Gary Rees, whose outstanding performance for the Midlands against the All Blacks was repeated on the England tour of South Africa.

Basically, I have selected the Grand Slam XV, with Alan Old being promoted from the bench to fly-half. Of course, my captain has to be Bill Beaumont, but he would also acknowledge three other outstanding leaders in the pack. Peter Wheeler is someone whose leadership I have enjoyed in club and representative matches – and Fran Cotton really impressed me when he led the North and Midlands against the 1976 Argentinians. Bill is first choice, with those two and Roger Uttley not far behind.

13

GETTING TECHNICAL

Despite the many efforts of rugby's law makers to lessen the role of the goal-kicker, the man with the big boot still rules. Strangely, some blame goal-kickers for that situation, but why should we be castigated for something we're good at? I have worked bloody hard to be one of the best goal-kickers in the world – people forget that I was first capped as an attacking full-back and was not even the number one kicker in the England team. It was four and a half years after my international debut before I first kicked for my country.

What makes a good goal-kicker? It's difficult to say – there is no photokit for the perfect exponent. They have come tall and short, thick and thin; some have a round the corner style, others kick with the toe; kickers from the pack, kickers from the backs, some kicking with great deliberation, others trying to add penalty points as quickly as possible. Some rub their boot on the back of the other leg, others throw grass to check the wind direction; some take two or three paces, others a wide arcing run; some run up with their gumshield in their hands, others don't take it out; some always face the target, others turn their backs before taking aim again; some look confident, others nervous; some achieve their goal and quietly jog back to halfway (I, allegedly, waddle), others are more exuberant; some are put off by the weather, others by a simple early miss; some dig a hole for the ball, others tee it up in a golf fashion; some aim for between the posts, others hit the ball wide and wait for wind to bring it in.

I hope that the pictures in this chapter will say more than a thousand words, but even they are meant as no more than a general guide. Just as in a golf swing, it is normally easy to spot a flaw which causes repeated failures, but within the premise of kicking a rugby ball between the posts and over the bar, there are endless variations of style and technique. There are basics to remember, for example keep your head down and make sure the non-striking foot is along-side the ball. But most all you have to find a style that works for you; and having done that constant practice will keep the points ticking over.

Again, it's important to get the conditions right. There's no value in kicking on the training field with a leather ball if when you play you use a plastic-coated one. And there's little point practising in a sheltered environment when your club's pitch is in the wide open spaces. As in cricket and most other sports, some days the ball just will not go where you want it to; then you have to fall back on your technique and work your way back. Those hoping to find a secret way to goal-kicking success in these pages are going to be disappointed.

Timing is all important. Having got into a routine, you must not allow yourself to be hurried out of it. Opponents often stand as close as they can and tilt to one side, or after letting you take aim, move a few steps to the side, but I don't think that has ever affected me. Some kickers can be put off by the ball toppling over, others prefer to have a member of the side holding the ball in wet and windy conditions. Every kicker has his personal ritual, some obviously get on the crowd's nerves as they slowly line up the ball and carefully step back. But the ritual is the routine which makes you arrive at contact with the ball in the best possible condition. It's much easier for a round-the-corner kicker to shuffle and repair a bad run-out than it is for a toe-kicker; he has to be spot on. I think the days of the toe-kicker are over; I do hope, though, that the practice will not become obsolete because, while there are many ways of putting the ball between the posts, rugby has few better sights than an orthodox toe-kicker on top form.

1a   1b

Points-scoring the Hare way. These sequences are meant as a guide and obviously there are many variations within them. But some essentials must be observed. In the run-up, you must keep your eyes on the ball and once you have made contact, the head must stay down as in *1d* and *2f*. Lifting your head is as much a failing with goal-kickers as it is with golfers. Sticking one's tongue out (*1a, c* and *d*) does not make the ball go any further or straighter but if it helps concentration there's no harm in it. Obviously, you have taken aim before starting your run-up. Some like to do this when setting the ball up and then take two or three steps to the side before embarking on their curving run. Again practice will tell you what is best. But you must put the non striking foot alongside the ball (*1c, 2e*). If you are not balanced correctly on your non-striking foot, then not only are you likely to make a mess of the kick, but you will probably fall over if the conditions are at all slippery. As

2a   2b   2c

1d

u can see in the run-up photographs, the left arm is also held out for
lance (*1b, 1c, 2d, 2e*). The way you finish up is equally important; how the
ll travels through the air is affected by the follow-through. Although I kick
ccer style, I don't regard myself as a round-the-corner kicker because with
traight follow-through I can cut out most of the curl on the ball's path. And
u use different kicks from different positions. Close in I tend to chip the
ll, so that with a limited follow-through I can reduce the margin of error.
n the left-hand side the draw will help give a bigger target, while on the
rong' right-hand side, you try to keep the ball straight to prevent it curling
ross the front of the posts. One of the main reasons for the current vogue of
cking with the instep instead of the toe is that the greater contact area with
e ball again reduces the margin of error, especially in the wet.

2e   *2f*

165

3a   3b   3c

Punting the ball is also a question of balance and keeping your head dow
but you have an added worry that is not present in place-kicking – t
position of the ball. If the ball is not dropped correctly on to the fo
(dropped and not thrown into the air, followed by an almighty swing) th
you are not going to be able to use the shape of the ball to spin it through t
air to get the maximum distance. And it's not a question of thumping t
ball, rather kicking through it. Again the left arm is used as balance (3
Personally, I like to lean back slightly when striking the ball (3e), but th

4a   4b   4c

3e   *3f*

:p my head down and straighten up in the follow-through. Again, the leg
uld swing through as high and straight as possible (*3f*). The pictures
ow show that a goal-kicker's life is not always a happy one. I may be
ebrating a penalty against Wales (*4a*), but the other photographs show me
ling the ball over when it is straying dangerously near the posts. Picture *4c*
ches me at my worst, when a succession of penalties went wide of the
get in the 1984 Calcutta Cup game. But picture *4e* was a penalty that I
naged to steer over via the post for a 13-13 draw against Wales in 1983.

4e   *4f*

167

14

SOUTH AFRICAN DIARY

Sunday 13 May

I travelled from Newark to London by train. Actually, because of a new British Rail timetable the train was supposed to go straight through the station without stopping. Just as Paul Dodge and I were wondering what we were going to do, we learned that an exception would be made for a couple of England players.

Lesley, as usual, had done my packing – I'm never sure what to take and I used to end up with too much in the early days – now I travel as light as possible. Going on an England tour is a great honour. This is my fourth England tour in six years. In 1979 it was the Far East, 1981 Argentina and 1982 the USA and Canada. In 1980, I missed out on the Lion's trip, but was adequately compensated by going on the Leicester centenary world tour to Australia and Fiji. In 1983, at my fourth attempt, I joined the British Lions' party for the visit to New Zealand. As events turned out, I may as well not have bothered. I appreciate that I'm very fortunate to travel the world at the expense of others, but sacrifices do have to be made. It's not easy leaving a young family, especially for a three-month tour. So as I set off for South Africa Donna and Christopher were not keen that I was disappearing again. This trip is only for four weeks, but it was difficult to explain that to them. Christopher did not cope well with my absence last summer and it doesn't help when things are not going well 12,000 miles away. There I was, being cold-shouldered by the Lions' selectors who didn't seem to want me around, with Lesley back at home telling the kids that 'Daddy would be home soon'.

Seven Leicester men played in England's match against Ireland, but only three of us are making this tour. Peter Wheeler, Clive Woodward, Rory Underwood and Steve Redfern are all unavailable. Paul and I were joined on the train by scrum-half Nick 'Spud'

Youngs and Ron Jacobs, the president of the RFU and the tour manager. For once England has two managers, Ron in charge of the tour and Derek Morgan, the chairman of selectors, looking after the team. We are not sure how this is going to work out, but it has looked like a case of over-manning from the start.

On the train we discussed the tour and then made our way to Twickenham to finish off our kitting out. There was a great air of secrecy about our getting together because Twickenham was worried that the anti-apartheid demonstrators might stage some publicity stunt. After collecting our gear at Twickenham, we sneaked off to our hideaway hotel. Then, in true undercover style, the party was assembled for a series of briefings about the tour, which included guidelines on how one should behave in the republic and our itinerary for the month ahead. Although assembled today, we are not leaving until Tuesday, which is rather strange seeing that there is a direct flight to Durban today. Had we taken that flight we would have had another couple of days to get acclimatised to the South African conditions, and besides, having left home you want to get on your way as soon as possible. When you've left the family for a month, they find it rather peculiar that you spend the first two nights in London.

Monday 14 May
We trained at Twickenham in the morning after the tour photographs were taken. There haven't been many surprises in the party: with Rory Underwood and John Carleton unavailable, Tony Swift and David Trick, who have both battled for Mike Slemen's left wing spot, now fight for the opposite flank. Steve Burnhill is a new face in the midfield while John Palmer came in when injury ruled out Bryan Barley. The surprise omission in the backs was that of Les Cusworth, who has been fly-half through the Championship and who was prepared to put his job on the line in order to go with England. In the event that gesture was not required.

Peter Winterbottom is the only back row forward from the game against Wales to have kept his place. John Hall, dropped for that game, had been brought back and the uncapped Gary Rees – a reward for his outstanding game against the All Blacks – Mike Teague and Chris Butcher have been introduced. John Scott has

169

taken over the captaincy and moved to the second row. He has been joined by veteran John Fidler and the uncapped Dave Cusani. The non-internationals in the front row are hooker Steve Brain and prop Malcolm Preedy. As well as the coach and two managers, the official party also includes president-elect Albert Agar, doctor Ian Duff and physiotherapist Kevin Murphy. Now, six months after the euphoria of our win over New Zealand, only six members of that victorious side are involved in this expedition.

The lads continued training after lunch, but I had been given permission to go and do some promotional work with Nike, which consisted of being photographed with Charlie Nicholas, Ian Botham, Christina Boxer and Ian St John for an advertisement which is coming out later in the year.

Tuesday 15 May
Today we leave for South Africa. Although you have been selected, trained with the lads and been kitted out, it's not until you are on that plane, with its wheels locked in the undercarriage, flying at 30,000 feet, that you feel you are on the trip for sure. Quite a few players who have been picked are not included in the official lists. Roger Uttley was vice-captain of the 1977 Lions, but he injured his back when the party were at Richmond and you will not find his name in the record books. Even in 1983 Donal Lenihan, the Irish lock, had to stay behind in London for a hernia operation as we set off. It was only Bob Norster's back injury which allowed Donal a second chance and the final fortnight in New Zealand.

We trained at Twickenham in the morning and then got ready for our late afternoon flight. I made the final phone calls home; after today chats with Lesley are going to be very expensive. (As it turned out, they were even more expensive than we had thought – the hotels in South Africa lumped on a hefty service charge for phone calls, which worked out at roughly 100 per cent.)

As we travelled by coach to Heathrow, the anti-apartheid protestors made themselves known. There were only about 30 of them, but they hurled abuse and threw leaflets at us as we rushed through a side entrance. It was all very dramatic, but rather unnecessary and trivial, I felt. For once England's rugby men travelled Gold Class. Normally we are stuck down at the back of the plane, which is not the perfect preparation for large sportsmen about to undertake an arduous tour. With a Lions' tour bringing in a cool two million, you would have thought that the men helping to bring in that bonanza would travel in style, but this isn't usually the case. With many of the forwards well over six feet tall, Economy Class is far from sufficient, especially as it seems we are expected to get off the plane and head straight for the training field. Fortunately, South African Airways upgraded us and so we travelled Gold Class; that's not First Class, but something similar to Club Class. The extra-wide seats and leg room make all the difference. The film on the flight was the latest James Bond – Roger Moore style – *Octopussy*, in which 007 as usual escapes several unlikely situations, a talent we will need to show in South Africa, if stories about their strength and our weaknesses are substantiated.

Wednesday 16 May
The flight took 14 hours and we landed at the Jan Smuts airport in Johannesburg at eight o'clock in the morning. There was a big crowd there to meet us, clapping and cheering. And, of course, this was our first taste of the TV cameras, photographers and Press men. There seemed a bigger turnout than there had been at Auckland Airport when we arrived with the Lions. Even now, it looks as if they are going to dog our steps all the way.

Because we had not taken the direct flight, we waited around Jan Smuts for a couple of hours before taking the plane to Durban. Once there, the coach took us to the Elangenei, a towering hotel overlooking the beach. But, as usual, there was not much time to admire the view. No sooner had we checked in and unpacked our stuff than Dick Greenwood had us running around King's Park. I could hardly breathe. The winds have come down from the Sahara, bringing an unrelenting dry heat which made me feel as though I was training in an oven. Dick worked us hard, determined to get the long journey out of our systems. A lot of us found the session tough going and were relieved when the coach called it a day.

I am sharing a room with Richard Hill and the pair of us were very grateful to have an early night, although I gather that some of the younger lads found some reserves of energy to take them on to the dance-floor of the 'Raffles' night-club upstairs.

Thursday 17 May

The team for the first match was announced this morning. Looking at the itinerary, the tour is really about the final three Saturday matches – Western Province and the two Tests. This opening Saturday is to be against a Currie Cup Section 'B' XV. With two games before the Western Province match, the first side is being viewed with great interest, although we have been told to read nothing into this. The management said it would be a mixed side. I hope so! If it's not I am in trouble because I'm not playing – I will be very unhappy if I am going to fulfil the role of dirt-tracker again. But with Peter Winterbottom and Nick Youngs also on the bench, I think maybe they are just looking at certain combinations. Steve Burnhill has made a mercurial rise to stardom and was probably not considered in the top dozen centres at the beginning of the season. Only two men – John Scott and Paul Rendall – remain from the England side that lost the last international to Wales.

There was another hard session, almost three hours, in the morning, and after lunch a few of us went to the Durban Park and aquarium. Durban is a favourite haunt of sharks and there have been frequent attacks over the years. Precautions are taken now to make it as safe as possible, but the aquarium itself has some spectacular sights. The dolphin show is always worth watching. However, not too many of us took the trouble to go and during a team meeting in the evening 'Scottie' pointed out that these trips are laid on for our benefit and that players would get more out of the tour if they bothered to take advantage of such diversions. Chris Butcher was pining a bit; the selectors have warned him off the beach, worried that our own 'beach bum' might tire himself out before the rugby.

The enormous accompanying media entourage has meant we are rarely off the TV or out of the sports pages of the newspapers. Yet to read the South African reports, it is the Springboks who are in trouble. There are endless discussions about who will be captain and who is going to play at fly-half. The early favourite appeared to be Gysie Pienaar, the former full-back who was outstanding against the 1980 British Lions. This evening we began our run of banquets and cocktail parties with a reception given by our hosts, the Natal Rugby Union. You get used to these occasions – some are more bearable than others. Generally, the people are polite and interested although there are those who are only concerned with telling you how great their rugby players are and how useless the English and British are.

Friday 18 May

Today we were taken into Zulu country to train and then spent the afternoon at a country club. Steve Burnhill has had some hamstring trouble and has withdrawn from tomorrow's match, letting in John Palmer to partner Paul Dodge. After three hard sessions, we were quite glad to get on the golf course. I partnered John Scott and we took on John Palmer and David Trick. There was a fair amount of hooking and hacking, but at least Dick Greenwood wasn't around to shout at us. The Bath boys were beaten, but I don't think we were much of a threat to Ballesteros and Watson.

Two years ago I went out to South Africa and took part in a goal-kicking competition with Andy Irvine, Naas Botha and others. Strangely, this was the first time that I had ever been involved in such an event. I had been really looking forward to it. It was organised by the Durban North Presbyterian Church in order to raise funds for an education centre. Sadly the top trio failed to do themselves justice and there was a play-off between local Cliff Brown and De Wet Ras. I was sorry for the crowd that we were not at our best in Tungay Park, but because the competition was held in open ground, and not in a big stadium like King's Park, the wind caused all sorts of problems.

Saturday 19 May

The day of the first match. It's always a relief to get the playing side underway. Durban is not exactly the ideal place to get into the big match atmosphere. I spent the morning on the beach, writing a letter and few postcards. There's nothing like this at home, certainly not near any rugby environment anyway – it is going to be difficult to shake off the holiday mood.

The large crowd at King's Park gave us a tremendous ovation as we entered the stadium. It was a moment I will savour for a long time – this was a sporting event which had nothing to do with politics. We got off to a winning start, 31-21, against a side that

173

included Errol Tobias at fly-half. Errol was the first coloured player to make the Springbok team, but the newspapers do not consider him as the likely fly-half for the Test team. England trailed just before the interval, but fought back. Yet, despite scoring four tries, our defence looked rather vulnerable and we let in three. Our scrummaging and first-time tackling – or rather lack of it – is something that Dick Greenwood is bound to work on in the next few days. But our final try, by John Hall, was a beauty, with some tremendous support play. Nick Stringer certainly put himself in the frame with a solid performance and banged over 15 points – I'll have to be on my toes on Wednesday against the Federation. In general, though, we made too many mistakes for an international team.

After the match, Dick took us dirt-trackers out for an hour's session, which was as hard as the match had seemed, and then we went back to the hotel to watch the highlights of the FA Cup final between Everton and Watford on TV. Everyone seemed relieved to have made a winning start. Back at the hotel, there was yet another reception at which we were entertained by a group of Zulu warriors. The lads that played were able to let off some steam, but those of us who are still waiting for our first match didn't feel able to relax in quite the same way. Now I am looking forward to my first serious rugby for nearly a month.

Sunday 20 May
We made our first move today, travelling from Durban to Cape Town. The day was wasted in a way because the flight wasn't until half past eleven. By the time we had got to Kimberley and then gone on to Cape Town it was after two o'clock. By the time all the luggage has been collected and we had taken the coach to Sea Point and checked into the Hotel President the afternoon had gone. It's a pity because Sunday is a special day on tour, and if you have to travel, it's better to to go in the early morning or early evening. Normally, the team will have played one of its harder matches the day before and it is the perfect time for the players to relax together. Often 'Sunday School' sessions – a lunch-time drink and sing-song – are compulsory. The 'Sunday School' was a tradition the 1983 Lions largely forgot about; if these don't happen naturally then the captain should instigate them, with a series of fines for non-attenders. All

this might seem childish and trivial, but such unity in times of exaltation – as well as in times of suffering – provides the backbone of team spirit.

I am rooming with John Hall, the young Bath flanker, as I did in London before we left. It seems as if they are giving me all the West Country newcomers to look after. John arrived in London for the trip with a fantastic black eye, which he had not, apparently, received on the rugby field. He won his first cap when he came on for Peter Winterbottom in the Calcutta Cup, but was hard done by when he was dropped after our defeat in Paris. John had not been happy with that and seems determined to prove the selectors wrong on this trip. After settling in we watched a video of yesterday's match. The star of the show was Chris Butcher, who kept shouting 'Go, Chrissie, go!' every time he saw himself catch the ball, and telling the rest of us not to watch when he missed a tackle or dropped the ball.

Monday 21 May
Training, as usual, this time at the Hamilton Rugby Club. The forwards concentrated on the scrummage, using a machine to practise against. At one point, Dick Greenwood asked for more fight, so when the pack broke up Phil Blakeway jokingly punched him in the stomach. He should have known better; soon there were rumours of disagreements between him and the coach.

The side for the second game was announced. All those who did not play on Saturday have been given a chance. Chris Butcher has retained his place at No. 8, with Mike Teague on the flank, so it is obvious that the management have him in mind for the Test spot. 'Butch' has attracted a lot of attention from the South African media, not only for his rugby. His carefree attitude is very reminiscent of that of Andy Ripley, who was a hit out here on the 1974 Lions' tour. We heard that Ewen Fergusson, the British Ambassador to South Africa who is a former Scottish international, has been instructed not to attend any of England's matches in line with the British Government's attitude to our visit here.

We went for lunch to the mayor's building in the centre of the town and in the afternoon made the perilous trip up Table Mountain. That journey up in the cable car may only take a few minutes, but it was one of the longest trips of my life. But that experience wasn't all that made me groggy; I feel as though I am going down with 'flu. Just what I don't need. If I drop out now, I might never get another chance. I took a few port and brandies and went to bed early after attending a cocktail party at the South African Rugby Board's headquarters at Newlands. Doc Craven was in full flight on his home territory, telling us that if their rugby players didn't get us, South Africa's 'fifth column' – their women – would. Albert Agar and Derek Morgan were missing – they went to watch the Springbok trials.

Tuesday 22 May
I didn't feel much better when I woke up. Still, the only thing to do was to try and run it off. We left Cape Town this morning and went off by coach to Stellenbosch where we are to play the Federation tomorrow. Stellenbosch is Doc Craven's headquarters and the university is in a breathtaking setting. Although the weather is fine, it has been raining for a week and the ground is heavy underfoot. What with that and my condition, my legs felt like lead and it was a strain to get through the session. Time is running out – if I don't feel better soon, I'll have to drop out; the last thing I want to do.

I decided to forget that problem for a few hours and enjoy the hospitality that had been laid on at the Stellenbosch wineries. They put on a superb meal for us – and even allowed the Press in too – it is very easy to forget the surrounding troubles in a place like this. After a very leisurely lunch, we took the coach back to our hotel. Most of the lads hung around the hotel in the evening, but I just had a few beers and went to bed, hoping for some improvement by the morning.

Wednesday 23 May
I had a restful night, but I still don't feel quite right. I didn't do much in the morning, just lazed around and went for a little captain's walk. I felt better and more confident as the coach took us up to Stellenbosch again. If I was going to sweat out the cold, this was the place to do it – it was absolutely baking.

The South African Federation team is made of of the coloured rugby players and others invited to bolster the scrum. The programme cover had action for England's match against the Federation in 1972 and the man with the ball – Errol Tobias – was in the side again today. Their back line was full of talent – Wilfred Cupido, Avril Williams and Hennie Shields. They took advantage of the hot and humid conditions and some sloppy defence to lead 21-10 just after the interval. Initially, it looked as if we were going to wipe the floor with them when Huw Davies made a 60-yard run only for Nick Youngs to drop the ball with the line at his mercy. That destroyed Nick's confidence for the remainder of the game and the rest of us weren't doing much better. I certainly wasn't covering myself in glory. Not only did I miss six kicks, but with the sweat pouring into my eyes, my defence was not as positive as I would have liked it to be.

Tobias was in even better form than he was on Saturday and scored 17 points including a try. Although we were trailing by 11 points early in the second half I was still confident that we could win. We were still five points adrift as the match entered the final ten minutes but then Tony Swift managed a try and finally I was given another penalty chance, which fortunately I put over for a 23-21 win. Still, the result was far from satisfactory and the situation wasn't helped when Paul Dodge went off with ankle trouble. Paul hasn't been back long after he broke his leg, so there are some worried faces about. 'Scottie' had some forceful points to make at the reception after the match, one of which was that this was the first time he had noticed a fork-lift truck in the line-out. This was a reference to the fact that the South Africans managed to make their jumpers seem weightless. Before John's few words, we had to endure a rather long speech by the Federation's President Mr Loriston.

I am not too happy with my form. I think they may well give Nick Stringer the spot against Western Province. But these uneasy contemplations rather paled into insignificance when I had a chat with the Federation's reserve full-back, one K. Paarwater. I was very flattered when he told me that he had just named his new baby son Dusty. After watching me that afternoon I was just glad that he didn't feel like changing his mind and calling him J. P. R. or Andy!

Thursday 24 May

We went down to train at the Newlands Stadium this morning. This is Western Province's ground – they are the Currie Cup champions, have many international players and are expected to be as tough an opposition as the Springbok Test team. 'Dodgy' feels a lot better, so any thoughts of sending for a replacement have been shelved for the present. Saturday's side was announced; I was very relieved to find myself there after yesterday. In view of the injury to Paul and Steve Burnhill's inexperience, Huw Davies will be partnered in the centre by John Palmer. Nick Youngs' display virtually handed Richard Hill his spot. Gloucester provided the front row and John Fidler, 'Scottie' and 'Butch' are in for their third successive games, as is Mark Bailey on the left wing, and Palmer. Our injuries are mounting. 'Scottie' is having trouble with his ankle and 'Fids' has amazed everyone with a hamstring injury. These problems are really hindering our preparation.

After lunch I went off with the manager, Ron Jacobs, to visit a farm just outside Cape Town. This was a very impressive place and seemed to have settled on the perfect combination. The farmer had sheep and grew wheat and plenty of vines – you can't do much better than that. While there was a relaxed atmosphere about the place, the set-up was fairly modern. The farmer also had his own personal 'zoo' with ostriches and zebras. But while accepting this as an almost perfect setting, I could not help my thoughts straying beyond these boundaries and to the more immediate problems and injustices of South African life.

Friday 25 May

I woke up with earache. I went to see Ian Duff, the doctor, who said that my ears were thick with wax. He put some drops in and said he would syringe them tomorrow before the game when the wax had softened up. We went back to Hamilton for our training this morning; 'Scottie' is still having trouble with his ankle and John Fidler wasn't able to take a full part in the session. 'Scottie' always seems to save his best for a tour. Both the 1980 and 1983 Lions would have benefited by his presence, but on each occasion Scotland's John Beattie was taken in his place. He certainly gave his all for us in Argentina in 1981; both ankles gave him a lot of trouble –

on his return he needed an operation to have artificial fibres put into them – plus he had terrible earache. He literally crawled out of his sickbed each match day, but that never showed on the field. His courage certainly impressed Derek Morgan, the manager on that trip, who has remained an important member of England's selection panel following that tour. John is doing a good job keeping the lads together. The players look to him more than to the coach or managers: Ron Jacobs is more than a generation away, while Derek's authority is rather weakened by the presence of Ron as co-manager. Dick has been coach for less than a year, and the players are finding him difficult to communicate with.

Saturday 26 May
I rose early and walked up the corridor to see if the doctor was about. He was, and he set about syringing my ears. The effect was sensational; once the bells had stopped ringing I could hear everything and my head was clear. I feel a lot better now and I am looking forward to the match against Western Province. After a week of near-perfect weather, the rains have come down. Today was a like a perfect English winter's day; suddenly we felt at home determined to show the South Africans that we are something more than the 'no-hopers' they have labelled us. The atmosphere was really tense for the first time on the tour; we knew enough about the South Africans' rugby to appreciate that the tough business was going to begin today. Not only were Western Province the Currie Cup champions, but the bulk of their team were bidding for places in the Springbok team which will be announced tonight.

At last, we have done ourselves justice. The result was a 15-15 draw, but the moral victory was ours. We led 15-6 at half-time and scored the only two tries of the afternoon through our Bath half-backs Richard Hill and John Horton. Richard has come on in leaps and bounds in less than a year of senior rugby. Now he is giving Nick Youngs no chance of finding a way back after his bad start at Stellenbosch. John Horton has been around for much longer, but after playing a key part in the Grand Slam, he was ignored in favour of first Huw Davies and then Les Cusworth. There were many who moaned about him kicking so much, but this was one of his best games for England. In the midfield John Palmer and Huw Davies knocked down every Springbok that moved. Our pack went really well and John Hall was outstanding in the loose. John Fidler was a dominant force in the line-out, while John Scott had the side well organised.

We should really have won but had to settle for a draw in controversial circumstances in the dying minutes. For once the Western Province winger, Carel du Plessis, found some space. David Trick came in to tackle him just as the South Africans kicked ahead. The pair were bundled over the touch-line. I looked worriedly at the referee, but Steve Strydom, who had seen the whole incident, waved play on. Then the opposition drew his attention to the touch-judge, who had his flag raised. We were astounded when, after a brief consultation, he gave them the penalty which Calla Scholtz put over to level the scores. To say we were slightly aggrieved would be a major understatement. There was nothing the touch-judge saw that the referee didn't. Originally, Strydom hadn't considered the tackle worth a penalty, but seemed to bow to the demands of the crowd, who were upset at the way their heroes had been performing. Surprisingly, that same touch-judge was looking the other way when our prop Malcolm Preedy was raked on two separate occasions.

All the same, our mood was really buoyant after the match at the reception at Newlands. The place was packed out and suddenly everyone was talking optimistically about our chances in the Tests. The Springboks seemed shocked that we had caused their champions any trouble at all. Back at the Hotel President where we had a dinner, Derek Morgan told the Press that Bryan Barley was to fly out as cover for 'Dodgy'. Paul's ankle hasn't been progressing as well as everyone hoped, but the management still want him about to bid for a Test place. The Springboks announced their Test team. It was no surprise to us that Errol Tobias will be the fly-half, but all the news is centred around the selection of Gerrie Sonnekus at No. 8. He is the loose forward that South Africa tried to turn into a scrum-half for the third Test against Willie John McBride's Lions in 1974. That was a big mistake and as a result he has spent ten years in the wilderness. The captain will be Western Province flanker Thuens Stofberg, and eight of his team-mates, four backs and four forwards, have also been selected. Schalk Burger, who won a lot of line-out ball for the South African Federation, has been brought into the second row. It looks a pretty impressive line-out to us, but not quite as daunting as it might have appeared this morning.

The evening was enjoyable; the events of today have given us something to build on. The night finished with a good old sing-song in the bar. Now, after a couple of false starts, the tour is really underway.

Sunday 27 May
After a week in Cape Town, we packed this morning for the move to East London for the South African Rugby Association match. It's amazing how much stuff you seem to collect on tours and there's always a great problem packing at the end of a long visit. Laundry is another hassle on tour. When you have seven days in one place it's not so bad because you can be sure of getting your clothes back. But when the stay is only a few days, then you are better advised to keep your laundry until you can be certain there will be time for it to be returned. Otherwise you are rushing around trying to find it before leaving.

At lunch-time, we held our first serious 'Sunday School'. Everyone joined in, which is the only way it works well. England teams have always been good tourists; they don't drift into cliques or keep themselves to themselves. They are happy to mix and everybody in this party, from the management downwards, gets on. After a few more songs, we took the bus to the airport to find that our plane had been delayed. Hanging around is always the biggest bugbear of any tour; the lads got a little boisterous at the airport and on the plane and one or two got a ticking off. One who didn't, at least not that time, was Steve Brain, who'd gone missing. Derek Morgan explained that he'd been given permission to see some family friends. On the way to the airport, their car had broken down. 'Brainy' is fast emerging as a real character; even now, though, he has not been officially posted as going AWOL.

It was early evening by the time we got to the Holiday Inn at East London. After the glamour of Durban and Cape Town, East London looks a little dull and the hotel isn't as classy as the previous two we have stayed in. For once I am on my own – my room-mate is to be

181

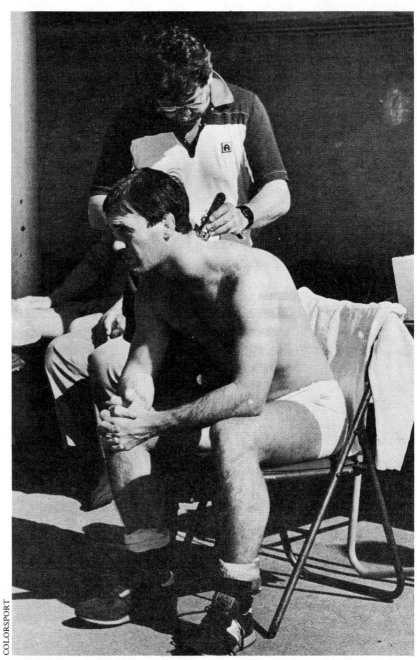

COLORSPORT

Steve Brain, the Coventry hooker who forced his way in to the second Test team, certainly caused some Cane (voted top tour drink) damage around South Africa.

Bryan Barley who is due to arrive tomorrow. Most people are just glad to be avoiding David Trick whose snoring is creating new records in South Africa.

Monday 28 May

Our tour is still making the front pages of the morning papers. Today they carried reports of what the English 'Sundays' thought of our performance against Western Province. Both South Africans and New Zealanders spend a lot of time reporting on what others think of them – and not only on the rugby field – which suggests a basic insecurity. Anyway, the band of travelling British journalists seemed in agreement that we had been robbed and even 'cheated'. That was not the only sporting story from back home. There was a report on Zola Budd's participation in the British Championship at Cwmbran and the accompanying demonstration by 20 Welsh anti-apartheid followers. The South Africans we have come across certainly don't regard Zola as any sort of traitor or defector and don't think of her as British. Most see this as the only way she can get into the Olympic Games and if she can do well there, then it will reflect glory on South Africa. But the longest running story so far on the trip is the alleged heavyweight title fight between Larry Holmes and Gerrie Coetzee. Nearly every day the venue and date seem to change as another promoter comes up with a better deal. Boxing, athletics and rugby are not the only sports causing interest. The South Africans are delighted at the news that Allan Lamb has been included in England's 13-man squad for the one-day internationals against the West Indies.

We trained at the ground in the morning. My back was not too good and I only had a light work-out. My back has become something of a source of amusement amongst the journalists, who have seen it interrupt my hard preparation in Canada, the USA, New Zealand and Argentina as well as France and the home countries. Just as Chalkie White used to say that lambing always seemed to occur on training night, the journalists now gauge how tough a session has become by the seriousness of my back problems.

Steve Brain was expected to arrive first thing this morning, but didn't turn up until later in the day. Bryan Barley did jet in on time, however, and went straight into action. He trained under floodlights and is in the team for tomorrow's match. Eleven changes have been made from Saturday's side – only Trick, Scott, Davies and Hall remain. Those who didn't play on Saturday are going to have to work hard now to force their way into the Test team.

This afternoon we went out on a coach trip. First we passed through a township. Some of the houses didn't look too bad, but others resembled little more than dog kennels. Then we travelled to the Ciskei, one of the 'homelands'. These are so-called independent states to which the coloureds and blacks are 'repatriated'. By the time South Africa gets around to giving everyone the vote, the majority in South Africa itself will be white because all the natives will have been safely housed in their 'homelands'. Fortunately, other countries refuse to recognise these places as independent states, basically because they are totally dependent on South Africa for their existence and their governments are anything but free to determine their own future. Not surprisingly, none of these 'homelands' seem to be situated in any of the wealthy areas of Southern Africa. We visited the Houses of Parliament in the Ciskei, outside which was a row of BMWs which belonged to the MPs. They – unlike the rest of their people – do not seem to be doing too badly. Then we went to the Bisho Independent Stadium where we were greeted by songs and traditional dancers. At least by travelling here we are seeing the situation at first-hand. Even the South African Rugby Board cannot supply us with rose-coloured glasses to wear at all times.

Tuesday 29 May
We woke up to Zola Budd on the front page of the *Daily Dispatch* again – this time she had beaten the world junior 1500 metres record. There was a picture, also on the front page, of a smiling Bryan Barley being greeted by a smiling Derek Morgan. I don't think the team manager was in such a friendly mood when he caught up with Steve Brain later.

This morning the dirt-trackers and replacements were joined on Dick Greenwood's training run by the Press. We thought they had chickened out at first, but as we made our way to the beach they could be seen struggling out of their hotel a quarter of a mile down the road. One or two of the Press corps were quite impressive, but one particular ex-player, carrying a little weight, was left behind, stranded on the beach as we made our way back to the hotel.

The weather improved for the afternoon's match, which was attended by many of the officials of the Ciskei Government we had seen the day before. Again, the BMWs were out in force. During the game I helped Ian Robertson with the radio commentary, interjecting with comments and assessments. It was good fun, although I would have enjoyed it more had England been in better form. Nobody did much today to suggest that they might break into the side that drew with Western Province. England got off to a perfect start, with ten points on the board in as many minutes. But Nick Youngs' try and Nick Stringer's two penalties did not herald the massacre that had looked inevitable earlier on. David Trick got another just before half-time, so we turned round 16-4 in front. We added three more tries after the interval for a 30-8 victory. Strangely, we conceded two more tries – the only side that has not breached our defence has been the champions Western Province.

By the time we got back to our hotel, East London had been plunged into darkness because of a power cut. We were all wandering around with candles, like some huge Christmas procession. But there was just enough light to enable us to witness one of the funniest events of the whole trip – John Scott being interviewed by a woman journalist. The Press always seem to send along people who know absolutely nothing about rugby, and this one was in rather a predicament when 'Scottie' pinched her list of questions. At that point he went into a long monologue, answering his own questions in graphic detail. Rather than enter into the spirit of the scenario (by now she had an audience of a dozen or so) she became agitated, a feeling which was not lessened when somehow a candle got entangled with her papers and they went up in flames. Instead of seeing it through, she turned on her heels and disappeared into the night. Our behaviour might sound boorish, but it's a method of self-defence. The regular journalists that travel with the team usually know when to draw the line, what is on and what is off the record. Others, often not even sports journalists, use guerrilla tactics. They come into the bar for a couple of hours and then repeat everything they've heard – or often overheard – and make a big name for themselves. Now they usually face an initiation ceremony, a trial

185

just to see what they are made of. If they have any character, they'll stick it out.

That power failure caused more than one journalist's agitation. It meant that this evening there would be no *Dallas* – a great favourite even in East London. We retired to the bar. The hundreds of candles gave the place a character that isn't evident in electric light. There we had a good old sing-song and probably the best night of the tour.

Wednesday 30 May
Another early start; this time for the nine o'clock flight to make the 35-minute journey to Port Elizabeth. The first real build-up to a Test is the announcement of the team. We went straight from the airport to training, waiting for the 15 names to be read out. But, back to traditional English ways, all we were told was that the side was being delayed and that we would be told tomorrow. There seemed to be no reason for this; everybody was expecting the same Saturday team and all it meant was that a valuable training session, in which the Test team could have got some necessary organisation done, was lost.

This evening the five Bath lads went out with some of the British Press on the winnings made by the *Daily Mirror*'s rugby correspondent Chris 'Mincer' Lander. Early in the season, he thought Bath were a good bet for the John Player Special Cup – and he was right for once, despite an injury-time scare when a Stuart Barnes penalty just missed in the final.

Most of us hung around the hotel where physio Kevin Murphy was busy as usual. 'Smurf' is one the great characters of rugby, and he was a great help to me in New Zealand with the Lions. He spends all his time looking after the lads and his room invariably looks like the casualty ward of a local hospital. England have been lucky with their physios – Don Gatherer is another who puts the players first. Last season I broke my hand against Bedford a week before the match with Wales. I had some X-rays and it was discovered there was a break; luckily Don looked after me and the word went out that I had a badly bruised hand. As it was I played without an injection and there was no problem; but had Don let on, I may well have had to withdraw from the team. Norman Collins is the man who looks after me back home; he's the 'miracle worker' at Nottingham Forest. Without him I would not have made the 1979 John Player Cup final against Moseley. Norman is a Welshman and he worked to get me ready for England's trip to Cardiff in 1981; he is always undecided about who to support, but on that occasion he thought the result was about right: 'My player scored 19 points – my country managed 21'.

Thursday 31 May
The sun was shining brightly as we made our way to the university field for our session in the morning. Our hotel is next to the beach and this is the start of a two-day break. The holiday atmosphere is certainly not conducive to the build-up to a Test match. After a quick work-out we at last learned of the team for the match. There were no surprises as the same side that drew with the Currie Cup champions have been asked to repeat their form. The team certainly has a West Country flavour with four of the front five coming from Gloucester and five Bath men in the side. That means new caps for Chris Butcher, John Palmer, Richard Hill, Mark Bailey and Malcolm Preedy. Only four men remain from our last international – a defeat by Wales at Twickenham. The news is also out that Paul Dodge is to return home as he has lost his fight to get fit again on the tour. It is a grave loss because he is one of our most experienced men and we are not doing so well that we can afford to let him go. Not all the side are that fit – both Huw Davies and John Hall are down with 'flu. I am pleased that John Palmer has an England place at last – it is six seasons since he arrived on the England bench and he must have wondered if his chance was ever going to come. All week the South Africans have been in a state of shock about our draw with Western Province and this has stirred memories of England's 1972 visit, during which the first ever whitewashed Championship side came here and beat the Springboks 18-9 in the only Test.

After training, a golf match was arranged against the Press. This was supposed to be a big affair, but many of the journalists had to go back and work because of the late announcement of the Test team. Anyway, I was paired with John Scott again and we did battle against the BBC's Ian Robertson and Nigel Starmer-Smith. They beat us on the last green, but the match was even overall.

187

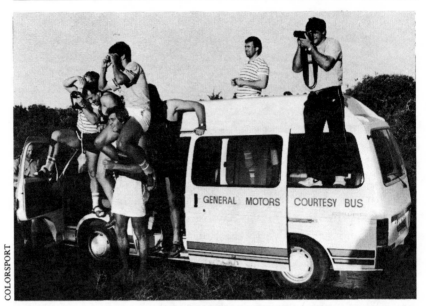

COLORSPORT

BOB THOMAS

A tour of lost causes, no more so than in Paul Rendall's pursuit of the elephants in Port Elizabeth, but at least he had something to chew on.

188

The rest of the lads went on a Land Rover around a safari park, but the expedition was something of a failure. Paul Rendall, the tour judge, moaned not only about the fact that the Land Rover had no shock absorbers, but also that all he saw in nearly two hours was the backside of a solitary elephant about a mile away. As they drove past steaming elephant droppings their guide became more and more excited, claiming that there must be elephants in the vicinity. The judge reckoned he kept seeing a native with a bucket pouring boiling water over the dung-heaps just before the Land Rover arrived and that the whole trek was a set-up.

Tonight the TV carried details of Spurs' arrival in South Africa. They are on their way to Swaziland to play a series of matches against Liverpool. It is a way of getting round FIFA's ban on players travelling to South Africa. All that will happen is that their supporters will make the journey into neighbouring Swaziland for their soccer entertainment, just as people go to Sun City for the illegal pastime of gambling and mixing with other races. For us in the Elizabeth Hotel, there are no such luxuries during the holiday – even the hotel bars are shut which is a real nuisance. Not because we are in desperate need of drink, it's just that we have nowhere to go but the public areas of the hotel, and everyone has something to say as they pass by. All these interferences are not helping our build-up to the Test.

Friday 1 June
I had a lie-in and then went to train on some ground near the beach in the late morning. *The Argus* reckons there is a question-mark over the 'Boks and that England's no-hopers are set to repeat a surprise win, but cricket has grabbed the headlines in the shape of Viv Richards, who has scored an amazing 189 against England, one of the greatest innings ever, even if it was in one-day cricket. All morning the TV had live coverage of the Comrades Race, one of the biggest annual sporting events in South Africa. It was won for the fourth successive year by Bruce Fordyce, who covered the 90 kilometres in just under five and a half hours for a new record. One year they run from Durban uphill to Maritzburg, the next downhill. This is a downhill year, but many of the runners – and there are thousands – claim they prefer the uphill run.

189

After running through our moves and how we are going to organise ourselves tomorrow we spent the rest of the day relaxing. In the afternoon I wrote my final letters and cards before going home, while others went to the races. All the forecasts have predicted wind and rain for the match, but the weather has not yet broken. Again, we found little peace in the hotel and retreated to the restaurant to turn our thoughts to the task in hand. The mood of the side is fairly confident, although we realise that we will have to play even better than last Saturday if we want a result.

Saturday 2 June

Another international day dawned. Suddenly the nerves appear as you worry about that first kick to touch, as everything goes through your mind. In the morning we went on our captain's walk. It was a real struggle getting out of the hotel, which was heaving with Afrikaners shouting what they thought were 'funnies' at us. I suppose it does help us get in the right mood for the job of beating their rugby team. After our walk, the weather still lovely and sunny, we had our team meeting and discussed plans for this afternoon. Looking at the papers, I was surprised to see that I am the second most experienced man on the field after John Scott. As for the match, after giving the Springboks a start, we fought back to level the scores early in the second half. I even had a long penalty chance to put us ahead for the first time, but the floodgates opened up in the final quarter of an hour with tries from Danie Gerber and Rob Louw which left us 15-33 adrift. Our defence was certainly not as solid as it had been against Western Province and the Springboks needed no second invitation to take even half chances. I suppose the biggest worry was that yet again England never really looked like scoring a try. I had managed four penalties out of six attempts, but was outshone by the South African full-back Johan Heunis, who contributed 21 points for his country.

I felt very low after the match. At the reception John Horton and I went and grabbed a few bottles of beer and sat at the back of the university hall, well away from everybody else. That may sound rather anti-social, but we weren't really in the right frame of mind for social chit-chat. We certainly weren't in the mood for any backchat, either, and there was plenty of that as we tried to get up

190

the stairs at the hotel. The place was throbbing with drunken supporters, all delighted at our demise, and there was a lot of pushing and shoving on our way up the stairs. The lads were not too happy with that.

Most of us gathered in the restaurant for a meal – it was also a safe refuge, well away from the hassle. The bars opened today after being closed for the two days' holiday and the locals were certainly making up for lost time. One or two of the lads tried to have a drink in the Oyster Bar, but the drunks were just looking for an excuse to cause the England team even more trouble. Most of us discussed the events of the day over a meal and then went up to the team-room to unwind on our own.

Sunday 3 June

By the time I started moving around, the hotel had appreciably quietened and emptied. I had a latish breakfast and then rang home. Then I packed my bags for the final move of the tour to Johannesburg. Our flight wasn't until two o'clock, so there was time for a short 'Sunday School' session. At this John Scott worked very hard to raise the spirits of the lads, especially the younger members of the party. He stressed that there were still another seven days to go and we had another chance to redeem ourselves; it was no use giving up. The lads seemed in better heart as we landed at Jan Smuts airport. We reached at the Landdrost Hotel early in the evening. When we arrived I found out that I will be sharing a room with the supposedly notorious Chris Butcher. After all I have been reading about him on this tour, I wonder whether an old-timer like me will be able to stand the pace of this final week.

Monday 4 June

The weather was sunny in Johannesburg this morning. People are telling us that all last week the temperatures were below freezing – at least we don't have to put up with that. We went along to the magnificent Ellis Park stadium for training in the morning. Our defeat on Saturday has certainly given those not in the Test team something to play for.

'Scottie' will again be captain against the South African Country XV at Sasolburg – that means the skipper will have played in all

191

seven matches. Considering he is also having to cope with a change of international position after six years, 'Scottie' is doing a tremendous job in trying to keep the team's spirits up. Some of the younger team members have taken the Test defeat pretty badly, but the captain is making sure that they don't spend too much time brooding about it. Only Scott, Trick, Horton and Butcher remain from the Test team for tomorrow's game. 'Butch' looked a little lost in the Test and will need a good performance to keep Mike Teague out of the reckoning. Derek Morgan said after the team was named that all 15 Test places were up for grabs.

John Scott's problems have continued – today he had to have his wedding ring cut off during training. He had a badly swollen finger from Saturday but didn't think his wife Oonagh would be too pleased when she heard the news back in Cardiff. Other wives have been in touch because some English newspapers have called us 'cowboys' and have suggested that we are having one big party. This eventually led to one or two noisy disagreements between the party and the journalists, but nothing that wasn't smoothed over later.

Tuesday 5 June

We set out quite early for the match at Sasolburg, which is about 50 miles from Johannesburg. It is an industrial area, not one of the prettiest rugby venues I've ever been to. Although the match was played in powerful sunshine, there was a very strong wind blowing downfield. Even walking about the field before the start, I knew that it was going to affect the game fairly seriously.

A lot of the journalists were critical after the match, but I thought the lads put together a very worthwhile performance. With the team needing time to settle, 'Scottie' decided to play against the wind. There was no score for half an hour as we tried to get ourselves together – as well as to contain the Country XV, who in some ways had little more than nuisance value. England turned round 4-0 in front, thanks to a Steve Brain try. We opened up a bit in the second half with five more tries, eventually winning 33-12. There was not too much running rugby, but it was a good, solid club performance giving us the conclusive victory we need. The star of the afternoon was Chris Butcher, who responded to the threat of losing his newly-won Test place with his best show of the tour. Although it was our biggest win of the trip, I don't think it was the sort of performance which will thrust many outsiders into the Test team. Nick missed his first five kicks at goal, so I feel reasonably sure that my place is secure. After the match there was the inevitable reception; we are beginning to grow a bit fed up with these, especially this evening when we had that long journey back to Johannesburg.

Wednesday 6 June

As happened last week, the Test team was not picked today. We trained at a local club and then went off to a game reserve. We thought it would be a quiet day out, but there was a barbecue lunch which was crawling with local dignitaries. The game reserve was very impressive, but I have been there before when I was over with the World XV. The building was covered with photographs of teams that had visited, so it is obviously a regular port of call for touring parties.

Several of the lads are struggling to throw off injuries, although all hope to be fit. Steve Brain has trouble with his back, Chris Butcher with his groin, Nick Youngs with his neck, John Fidler with his ankle and Mark Bailey is worried about his hamstring. Again it was a day which could have been spent organising the Test team. Considering that most of our followers have written us off, the spirit is very good within the party. Whilst appreciating that we have a tough job ahead, there is a real feeling that we can win the second Test. 'Scottie' heard that his club Cardiff's tour of Barbados, scheduled for later in the summer, has been called off because of the Welsh Rugby Union's decision to retain sporting links with South Africa. 'Scottie' was not due to go on the trip himself, but now wonders whether they will go anywhere. (In the end they went to Bangkok!)

Thursday 7 June

We trained at Ellis Park today. The team has still not been announced and the management concentrated on scrummage practice, which suggests some changes might be made there. When the side did come out, the major shock was in the front row where the Gloucester front trio have been thrown out *en masse*. They will be replaced by Paul Rendall, Steve Brain (who is 'over the moon') and

193

Gary Pearce. The other change is the dropping of David Trick for Tony Swift. That is rather cosmetic, but the forward switch has taken nearly everyone by surprise. We were penalised heavily in the first Test by neutral French official Renee Hourquet for collapsing the scrum. Initially, we thought his presence would stop the Springboks' tricks in the line-out, but instead he turned out to be something of a 'homer' and constantly picked on us in the scrum although there seemed little reason to do so. That obviously worried our management who hope to stop the problems with a completely new front-row unit.

I spent a lot of the session practising my goal-kicking, trying to come to terms with the difference at altitude from sea-level. The ball goes further and you can actually feel that as you kick. I also had some of the other lads kicking to me because you need a different judgement on the High Veldt. You have to position yourself another ten yards back otherwise you find yourself desperately back-pedalling as the ball goes sailing over your head.

I am getting on very well with the infamous Butcher. The stories about him are very greatly exaggerated. After spending one night with him, I can report that he's not a big drinker; about four bottles of beer is his quota. To be fair, he has a fairly casual approach to life, having wandered around most of the world, but he's a very likeable lad.

Friday 8 June
We woke up to Zola Budd again. She blazed out of the front page of the *Citizen* with news of her place in the British Olympic team by virtue of winning the 3000 metre trial in a world record junior time. This morning it was off to Ellis Park again. The major fitness worries concern Bailey's hamstring and Fidler's ankle. The Press have jumped on to the dropping of Phil Blakeway, suggesting that there has been a personality clash between him and 'Scottie'. They certainly are two entirely different types of character, but there's no way that the captain would have left anyone out of the team if he thought he was worth a place. After the session, everyone was passed fit.

After lunch I went out shopping for presents for the family. It's always difficult in the final week of a tour to keep your mind on the job in hand. You are looking forward to getting home, but there is also the toughest match of the tour to play first. The more trips I go on, the harder it is to find the right sort of presents, especially for Lesley. The kids are growing up, so their ages generally dictate what kind of gifts they get. But the wife is far more difficult. In the end, I bought her a ring and a gold necklace.

During the day when we weren't training or shopping this week, the squad has spent a lot of time around the swimming pool. The weather has been really good. There has been a regular trail of South African journalists visiting us; most of them seem interested in talking to 'Butch'. This evening I did my best to relax by having a few beers. The Landdrost Hotel is certainly quieter than the Elizabeth and we are able to keep away from the general crowd.

Saturday 9 June

A day of disaster for English rugby. After a quiet morning, we made our way to Ellis Park. The mood was confident and we felt all right in the changing-room, which is not always the case. The preparation has been good – more thorough than in some matches this year. 'Scottie' said in his team talk that our defence must be solid and that we must not give tries away as before. That all went wrong. The Springboks came out and totalled us in the first 40 minutes. By then we were 22-3 down. The character of the side came through in the second half when we could easily have crumbled. Some critics said that the South Africans had eased up, but that was not my reading of the situation. Danie Gerber was in magnificent form in that first half and grabbed a hat-trick of tries. Try as we might there seemed no way to contain him. After we had calmed things down following the interval, the South Africans made a late rally for a record 35-9 victory. In both Tests we had conceded nine tries and scored none ourselves. I managed three penalties in the second Test, but they were never going to make much difference. As if that wasn't bad enough, Ellis Park has giant replay screens and the RFU hierarchy had given the home Board permission to show highlights during the game. This meant every try we conceded was flashed on the giant screen twice more. The replays didn't bother me; you don't really study them, but it's hard to keep them out of the corner of your eye when you are standing behind the try-line.

195

The reception was held at Ellis Park and being the final match of the tour everyone seemed to have their say. But I was not really in a listening mood. This is probably the worst I have ever felt coming off a rugby field. I have been beaten badly before, but never like this. This evening was one for drowning the sorrows, but, as often happens in these circumstances, it was more a time for reflection. Slowly, but surely, I began to come out of my depression.

Sunday 10 June
Fortunately, we got out of Jo'burg early on and went to visit a farmer, a friend of Ron Jacobs, and had a barbecue. This is just what we wanted; a few beers, away from everybody – this is the way to round off a tour. Slowly we recovered. Of course, there was the final court session of the tour, when those who have been dishing out punishments for three weeks find themselves on the receiving end. Poor John Scott, as captain, seemed to cop the lot and he was certainly in a tired and emotional state at the Jan Smuts this evening as we got ready to go home. It was the first time that 'Scottie' has let himself go on the trip; after all his responsibilities of the past weeks, nobody could blame him for letting his hair down. Still, the censorious grimaces of some committee men were visible as we boarded the jumbo home. Fortunately, John's sleeping potion worked perfectly and he was soon away. I was met by Lesley and the children at Heathrow and we went to the Penta Hotel for coffee and to pick up some things I had left there before the trip. Then it was home to reflect on some pleasant tour memories off the field and the hell on it.

15
POSTSCRIPT

No sooner had I announced my retirement from international rugby than the Press were speculating on my return to the England team. I had made up my mind in all honesty because the business on the farm was taking more and more time and I also felt the family warranted more consideration. My experiences in South Africa also had a bearing on my decision. But I was happy to carry on for Leicester and the Midlands, who met the touring Wallabies at Welford Road in 1984. Being involved at first-class level means that it is not inconceivable that I might find a way back to the England jersey, but for all concerned it would be better if that did not happen. Still, it's very difficult to refuse an SOS and coach Dick Greenwood was asking about my availability even before the Australian match, which England lost heavily.

Judging by the amount of time I have spent pursuing my sporting interests over the years, everyone imagines that I lead the life of a gentleman farmer. That's not quite the case and had it not been for my father's help over the years and the willingness of Richard Coy to work the weekends I was away, I couldn't have carried on. I suppose the summer is our slackest time and my farming season begins in August and September when I sell breeding sheep to local farms. At this time, we are also buying store lambs which we fatten up, either inside or outside. This buying goes on until December and we generally look for our livestock in North Yorkshire, Northumberland and the East Midlands.

How many we buy depends on the quality of sheep on the day – and the price of course. By Christmas we have started to sell our own fattened sheep and this goes on until the beginning of the summer. We also have a 'flying flock' of ewes which we buy in the breeding sales during August. These have generally been discarded by the big farms because they have lost their teeth and can quickly

FRANK TEWKESBURY

An everyday story of farming folk, with Donna on the prowl.

Christopher on the attack.

lose their condition. But we feed them mass silage and their rubbery old gums can cope. During the summer we also sell our fattened lambs from this 'flying flock' with the ewes – that's how they get their name. To people we meet as we travel the country, I'm still the Boy following his Dad; there's one dealer who always says that the first division is there when my father goes and that only the second has turned up when I'm in attendance.

We also keep a few cattle on the farm, which again we fatten up. Dairy farming is too much like hard work; you have got to milk the cows twice a day and they like their timetable to be spot on. It's not possible to say how many sheep we have on the farm at any one time, but the total runs into thousands. Our accountant is always rather disappointed that we can never put our finger on the exact figure. Sometimes you have to put in a long hard day and then most of the night, but the work is very satisfying and I can't imagine doing anything else. It's the quality of life which is important to me.

I've had my share of ups and downs, but I wouldn't change a minute of my rugby life. Even in the most horrendous defeat, the England lads have been great company, seldom allowing the most unfair pressures and behaviour to get them down. Maybe if we took things as personally as the Welsh do sometimes, then we might be a harder side to beat. But that's not our nature. There's a whole world outside rugby and that fact is put quickly into perspective when you are up half the night, helping a ewe with a difficult birth.

I've been lucky that my role of goal-kicker has thrust me in the spotlight, not always favourably; but records mean nothing. I know that one day my world points record and England tally will be beaten, just as Fred Trueman did when he set his total of 307 Test wickets. Trueman, though, replied that whoever passed his tally would be 'bloody tired'! It has not been the goal-kicking which has worn me out, more the travelling, training and general hassle in fighting battles irrelevant to what England have been trying to do on the field. But it has been worth it, a feeling I hope this book conveys. Peter Wheeler wanted me to entitle it *Rugby From Behind* as a companion volume to his *Rugby from the Front*. In many ways it might be, but at least I have not spent most of my Saturday afternoons with my head 12 inches off the ground. Maybe he should have called his *A Foot Apart*.

COLORSPORT

NEWARK ADVERTISER

Above: *'The gentleman farmer', although one of my cows steals the scene.*
Below: *My tree on South Clifton Green, with some of the Leicester men that made it possible for me to plant it:* (left to right) *Tim Barnwell, Tim Burwell, Peter Wheeler, Chalkie White, me, Clive Woodward and Paul Dodge.*

Peter's suffering at the hands of officialdom carried on into late 1984 after he was sent off along with Mark McBain in the Midlands-Australia match at Leicester. Because he had been dismissed with a tourist, the hearing was conducted in front of a disciplinary committee of the International Board. Despite the fact that he was to be judged by them, Twickenham lost no time in imposing their 30-day ban and suspending him from international rugby for the year – both automatic punishments. That made anything proposed by the disciplinary meeting superfluous – Wheeler was handed out the same ten-day ban as McBain. England have got themselves into a real mess with their policy of not considering sent off players for the season; Steve Bainbridge was also out of action in 1984-85 because of this. Not only has no other country followed this lead, but it is unfair because you could miss six England games or none, depending on when you are dismissed. And other countries are not slow to exploit England's strait-jacket, knowing that our forwards can only retaliate at their peril.

The Midlands should have beaten the Australians. We were in control until Les Cusworth went off with torn knee and ankle ligaments and then our skipper Peter departed. The Aussies immediately scored a try, then added two penalties for a 21-18 victory. Still, we had helped restore some English pride after the national side's humiliation at Twickenham three days previously when they went down 3-19. England had five new caps, including Nigel Melville, at last, as scrum-half and captain. But they lost control up front and never stood a chance . . . the lack of preparation was there for all to see. Then Australia went on to the Grand Slam.

A few weeks previously, there had been rumours of me turning to rugby league when Mansfield Town said they hoped to hear from me. Actually, when I announced my retirement, they sent me a letter asking if I would be interested in rugby league. If I was, I was to get in touch with them. I wasn't and merely put the letter away. Then several weeks later, the story came out – obviously somebody was looking for publicity. Having spent two afternoons in South Africa trying to tackle Danie Gerber, I don't really think my style would be suited to the rough and tumble of the league code. Rugby Union suits me right down to the ground and my size nine boots!

201

BOB THOMAS

Now get this straight you lot! Unfortunately, the forwards took very little notice of my advice.

CAREER STATISTICS

Dusty Hare: Record England Points

Year	Venue	Opposition	Score	Tries	Cons	Pens	DGs	Pts
1974	Twickenham	Wales	W 16-12	—	—	—	—	0*
1978	Parc des Princes	France	L 6-15	—	—	—	—	0*
1978	Twickenham	New Zealand	L 6-16	—	—	1	1	6
1979	Twickenham	New Zealand	L 9-10	—	—	3	—	9
1980	Twickenham	Ireland	W 24-9	—	3	2	—	12
1980	Parc des Princes	France	W 17-13	—	—	1	—	3
1980	Twickenham	Wales	W 9-8	—	—	3	—	9
1980	Murrayfield	Scotland	W 30-18	—	2	2	—	10
1981	National Stadium	Wales	L 19-21	1	—	5	—	19
1981	Twickenham	Scotland	W 23-17	—	1	3	—	11
1981	Buenos Aires	Argentina	D 19-19	—	2	1	—	7
1981	Buenos Aires	Argentina	W 12-6	—	1	2	—	8
1982	Parc des Princes	France	W 27-15	—	2	5	—	19
1982	Twickenham	Wales	W 17-7	—	—	3	—	9
1983	Twickenham	France	L 15-19	—	—	4	—	12
1983	National Stadium	Wales	D 13-13	—	—	2	—	6
1983	Twickenham	Scotland	L 12-22	—	—	3	—	9
1983	Lansdowne Road	Ireland	L 15-25	—	—	5	—	15
1983	Twickenham	New Zealand	W 15-9	—	1	3	—	11
1984	Murrayfield	Scotland	L 6-18	—	—	2	—	6
1984	Twickenham	Ireland	W 12-9	—	—	3	—	9
1984	Parc des Princes	France	L 18-32	1	2	2	—	14
1984	Twickenham	Wales	L 15-24	—	—	5	—	15
1984	Boet Erasmus	South Africa	L 15-33	—	—	4	—	12
1984	Ellis Park	South Africa	L 9-35	—	—	3	—	9
Individual scoring record				2	14	67	1	240

*Alan Old was the goal-kicker in these matches

Kickers' Points Table

	Tests	Pts	Avge
Andy Irvine (Scotland, Lions)	60	301	5.01
Ollie Campbell (Ireland, Lions)	29	243	8.37
Dusty Hare (England)	25*	240	10.43
Phil Bennett (Wales, Lions)	37	210	5.67
Don Clarke (New Zealand)	31	207	6.67
Allan Hewson (New Zealand)	19	201	10.57
Tom Kiernan (Ireland, Lions)	58	193	3.32
Jean-Pierre Romeu (France)	22	139	6.31
Bob Hiller (England)	19	138	7.26
Pierre Villepreux (France)	29	133	4.93
Piet Visagie (South Africa)	25	130	5.20
Peter Dods (Scotland)	11	124	11.27
Fergie McCormick (New Zealand)	16	121	7.50
Naas Botha (South Africa)	10	102	10.20

*Hare was not used as a goal-kicker in his first two internationals. Others, for example Irvine, were not always the first-choice kicker.

Note: Irvine's tally includes 28 points from nine Lions' Tests, Campbell's 26 from seven, Bennett's 44 from eight and Kiernan's 35 from four.
Dusty Hare is England's most-capped full-back with 25 appearances (Bob Hiller is next with 19 caps).
Dusty Hare is England's leading points-scorer with 240 (Bob Hiller is next with 138).
Dusty Hare scored all England's points on eight occasions: 6 v New Zealand (1978); 9 v New Zealand (1979); 9 v Wales (1980); 19 v Wales (1981); 15 v Ireland (1983); 6 v Scotland (1984); 15 v Wales (1984); 9 v South Africa (1984).

Record v Individual Countries

	Tests	Tries	Cons	Pens	DGs	Pts
Wales	6	1	—	18	—	58
France	5	1	4	12	—	48
New Zealand	3	—	1	7	1	26
Ireland	3	—	3	10	—	36
Scotland	4	—	3	10	—	36
Argentina	2	—	3	3	—	15
South Africa	2	—	—	7	—	21
Total	25	2	14	67	1	240

Record on International Grounds

	Tests	Tries	Cons	Pens	DGs	Pts
Twickenham	12	—	5	33	1	112
Parc des Princes	4	1	4	8	—	36
Murrayfield	2	—	2	4	—	16
National Stadium	2	1	—	7	—	25
Buenos Aires	2	—	3	3	—	15
Lansdowne Road	1	—	—	5	—	15
Boet Erasmus	1	—	—	4	—	12
Ellis Park	1	—	—	3	—	9

Results v Individual Countries

	Tests	Won	Drawn	Lost	For	Agst	Per cent
Wales	6	3	1	2	89	85	59.50
France	5	2	—	3	83	94	40.00
New Zealand	3	1	—	2	30	35	33.33
Ireland	3	2	—	1	51	43	66.66
Scotland	4	2	—	2	71	75	50.00
Argentina	2	1	1	0	31	25	75.00
South Africa	2	0	—	2	24	68	00.00
Total	25	11	2	12	379	425	48.00

Results on International Grounds

	Tests	Won	Drawn	Lost	For	Agst	Per cent
Twickenham	12	7	—	5	173	162	60.00
Parc des Princes	4	2	—	2	68	75	50.00
Murrayfield	2	1	—	1	36	36	50.00
National Stadium	2	—	1	1	32	34	25.00
Buenos Aires	2	1	1	—	31	25	75.00
Lansdowne Road	1	—	—	1	15	25	00.00
Boet Erasmus	1	—	—	1	15	33	00.00
Ellis Park	1	—	—	1	9	35	00.00

International Points

	Tests	Tries	Cons	Pens	DGs	Pts	Per cent
Dusty Hare	25	2	14	67	1	240	62.38
Rest of England	25	26	1	2	9	139	37.62
Total	25	28	15	69	10	379	100.00

International Points at Twickenham

	Tests	Tries	Cons	Pens	DGs	Pts	Per cent
Dusty Hare	12	0	5	33	1	112	64.73
Rest of England	12	11	1	2	3	61	35.27
Total	12	11	6	35	4	173	100.00

England Tours

	Year	Matches	Won	Lost	Drawn	For	Agst	Per cent
Japan, Fiji and Tonga	1979	7	7	0	0	270	93	100.00
Argentina	1981	7	6	0	1	193	100	92.94
USA and Canada	1982	8	8	0	0	352	34	100.00
South Africa	1984	7	4	2	1	145	160	66.06
Total		29	25	2	2	960	387	89.65

Hare's Points for England

	Tests	Tries	Cons	Pens	DGs	Pts
Major internationals	25	2	14	67	1	240
Other internationals	6	—	26	12	—	88
Other England games	7	2	17	18	—	96
All England games	38	4	57	97	1	424

Hare on Tour with England

	Tries	Cons	Pens	DGs	Pts
1979 v Japan (W 21-9)	—	2	3	—	13
1979 v Fiji Juniors (W 39-22)	—	1	2	1	11
1981 v San Isidro Club (W 20-14)	—	2	—	—	4
1981 v Buenos Aires Selection (W 34-15)	—	3	4	—	18
1981 v Argentina (D 19-19)	—	2	1	—	7
1981 v Argentina (W 12-6)	—	1	2	—	8
1982 v Canada (W 34-6)	—	3	3	—	15
1982 v Pacific Coast (W 28-6)	—	2	2	—	10
1982 v Mid-Western XV (W 58-7)	2	7	4	—	34
1982 v USA (W 59-0)	—	7	2	—	20
1984 v SARF (W 23-21)	—	—	5	—	15
1984 v Western Province (D 15-15)	—	2	1	—	7
1984 v South Africa (L 15-33)	—	—	4	—	12
1984 v South Africa (L 9-35)	—	—	3	—	9
Total (14 games) (P14 W10 D2 L2)	2	32	36	1	183

British Lions' Tour 1983

	Matches	Won	Drawn	Lost	For	Agst	Per cent
New Zealand	18	12	0	6	478	276	66.66

Hare with the Lions

	Tries	Cons	Pens	DGs	Pts
Wanganui (W 47-15)	—	3	5	—	21
Bay of Plenty (W 34-16)	—	4	2	—	14
Mid-Canterbury (W 26-6)	—	1	4	—	14
West Coast (W 52-16)	—	6	4	—	24
Southland (W 41-3)	—	1	2	—	8
Hawke's Bay (W 25-19)	—	2	1	—	7
Total	—	17	18	—	88

Hare was carried off injured in the last two matches, but was still undefeated in his six tour matches.

207

Representative Matches

7 Nov 1970	Midlands Counties East 14, Fiji 24 (Leicester) *(came on as replacement)*
13 Oct 1973	England Under-23 19, Japan 10 (Twickenham) *Hare: two tries, one penalty – 11 pts*
13 April 1974	Barbarians debut Cardiff 11, Barbarians 9 (Cardiff Arms Park)
5 Oct 1974	England Under-23 40, Tonga 4 (Twickenham) *Hare: four penalties, four conversions – 20 pts*
12 Nov 1975	Midlands Counties East 11, Australia 9 (Leicester) *Hare: one penalty – 3 pts*
9 Oct 1976	North & Midlands 24, Argentina 9 (Leicester) *Hare: one conversion, five penalties – 17 pts*
15 Oct 1977	England XV 37, USA 11 *Hare: five conversions, one penalty – 13 pts*
18 Nov 1978	Midlands 15, New Zealand 20 (Leicester) *Hare: five penalties – 15 pts*
3 Nov 1979	Midlands 7, New Zealand 33 (Leicester) *Hare: one penalty – 3 pts*
6 Oct 1982	Midlands 25, Fiji 16 (Leicester) *Hare: one try, two conversions, three penalties – 17 pts*
16 Oct 1982	England 60, Fiji 19 (Twickenham) *Hare: six conversions – 12 pts*
15 Oct 1983	England 27, Canada 0 (Twickenham) *Hare: three conversions, three penalties – 15 pts*
8 Nov 1983	Midlands 19, New Zealand 13 (Leicester) *Hare: one conversion, two penalties, one dropped goal – 11 pts*
6 Nov 1984	Midlands 18, Australia 21 (Leicester) *Hare: five penalties – 15 pts*